CASABLANCA

The Motion Picture

COCKTAILS

COCKTAILS

We'll Always Have Aperitifs

RECIPES BY CASSANDRA REEDER
WRITTEN BY S. T. BENDE

INSIGHT
EDITIONS

SAN RAFAEL · LOS ANGELES · LONDON

CONTENTS

JUE ZERO

NONALCOHOLIC DRINKS

LA PARTAGE

HORS D'OEUVRES & CANAPÉS

DEALER'S SIGNATURE

SYRUPS, MIXERS & SPICES

INTRODUCTION

Set amid the backdrop of the second World War, Michael Curtiz's Academy Award–winning 1942 film *Casablanca* opens with a map of Africa and closes as thick fog creeps across a Moroccan airstrip. The narrative bookended by these images is that of Rick Blaine, a bar proprietor with access to two letters of transit, which represent an escape route for hopeful refugees looking to start a new life in the Americas. Over the course of the film, Rick must decide if he'll use these exit visas to help his former love, Ilsa, escape with her freedom-fighting husband, Victor Laszlo. Shining a light on the experiences of those displaced by war, who "wait in Casablanca—and wait—and wait—", the film captures the loves lost, friendships found, and lives lived even when it seems like you are waiting for your story to begin.

Designed in partnership with the studio behind the iconic film, *Casablanca Cocktails* is a collection of handcrafted mixers, aperitifs, nightcaps, and canapés, along with inspiring behind-the-scenes insights into the making of the movie. Together, these elements celebrate the everyday moments that might not seem like they amount to a "hill of beans in this crazy world," but can, in fact, change everything. The recipes within these pages draw inspiration from the flavors beloved by the French patriots who populate Rick's Café Americain, the heady spices of the Sahara Desert, and the citrusy blooms that waft along the heat waves of Morocco's moonlit nights. They draw on ingredients that would have been popular in Casablanca at the time of filming, creating a memorable mix of historically inspired cocktails, nonalcoholic beverages, and culinary creations that might have been served at Rick's well-loved watering hole and brings them into the homes of movie lovers the world over.

Recipes are organized to follow the course of an evening spent at Rick's Café Americain, sipping drinks, placing wagers on roulette, and dreaming up futures made possible by those ever-elusive exit visas. Accordingly, the book begins with aperitifs, or Opening Bets, including recipes like Train to Marseille and As Thyme Goes By. The party continues with mid-evening pick-me-ups, and inches toward the end of the night with digestifs, or Finales, like The Poor Corrupt Official and We'll Always Have Paris. Just as a game of roulette has its Jue Zero variation, this book includes nonalcoholic options to accommodate patrons of all stripes. Along the way, this cocktail book takes readers on an in-depth journey through the libations and culinary creations that would have delighted the Allies, expatriates, and ever-hopeful refugees who gathered at Rick's Café Americain. Including more than seventy recipes, many paired with opportunities to peek behind-the-scenes at the making of the classic film, *Casablanca Cocktails* is designed to bring together friends, families, and fans of this epic love story. Each recipe is an opportunity to raise a glass to new memories and moments you'll always have to enjoy: from Paris to aperitifs.

EN PLEIN

TIMELESS CLASSICS

Often used in games of roulette, *En Plein* refers to a bet placed entirely upon a single number. It's done when one is so confident in the outcome of one's wager, no other gamble seems necessary. It's an appropriate theme for the recipes that follow—a series inspired by the "Timeless Classics" that have endured over the years to become every bit as iconic as *Casablanca* itself. From the Sidecar (page 20) to The Rickey (page 16), these beverages are sure to please any crowd.

FRENCH 75

When one of Rick's Café Americain's more problematic patrons, Yvonne, seeks to impress a certain German gentleman, she asks the bartender to prepare a row of French 75s. Yvonne's countryman balks at her decision to share a drink with the enemy but takes no issue with her choice of beverage. The French 75 is a well-loved tipple that's every bit as classic as *Casablanca* itself. Dry gin and lemon juice are sweetened with simple syrup, then elevated with a bubbly dose of Champagne. This light, citrusy beverage is guaranteed to cause a stir . . . just like Yvonne!

1½ ounces gin

¾ ounce lemon juice

¾ ounce Simple Syrup (page 150)

2 to 3 ounces Champagne or other sparkling wine, chilled

Lemon twist, for garnish

If desired, chill the serving glass in the freezer for 10 to 15 minutes.

In a cocktail shaker filled with standard, cubed ice, add the gin, lemon juice, and simple syrup.

Shake for 10 to 15 seconds until well chilled.

Strain into the serving glass, with or without ice, depending on your preference.

Top off with Champagne to fill the glass.

Garnish with a lemon twist.

Yvonne's choice of beverage could in fact have held a hidden meaning. The French 75 gets its name from the French 75 mm field gun—a fast-firing piece of field artillery used by the French Army during World War I and later, in World War II. Like its namesake weapon, this beverage packs a kick.

CHAMPAGNE COCKTAIL

In many respects, the freedom fighter Victor Laszlo and Casablanca's self-serving Captain Renault don't have much in common. One trait they do share: They are both fond of a particular Rick's Café signature specialty—the Champagne Cocktail. This version of the elegant elixir combines a bitters-soaked sugar cube with a sizeable splash of Champagne. Topped with a touch of cognac and served in a festive flute, the Champagne Cocktail will have even the most erstwhile of enemies toasting together. À votre santé!

1 sugar cube

2 to 4 dashes aromatic bitters

½ ounce cognac (optional)

3 to 4 ounces Champagne, chilled

Lemon or orange twist, for garnish

If preferred, chill the serving glass in the freezer for 10 to 15 minutes.

Drop the sugar cube into the serving glass.

Douse the sugar cube with the bitters and let it dissolve for 10 to 15 seconds.

Add the cognac, if desired, then top off with the chilled Champagne.

Garnish with a lemon twist.

KIR ROYALE

Casablanca's famed freedom fighter Victor Laszlo understood the importance of hope. He rallied Allied forces and encouraged resistance efforts even amid the expansion of enemy-occupied territory. While Laszlo worked tirelessly in the world of the film, a Catholic priest kept spirits raised in ours. Canon Félix Kir—a hero in his own right—helped over 4,000 prisoners of war escape to freedom. Like Victor Laszlo, he understood the power of hope . . . so when Nazi troops stole wine from the Burgundy region, Canon Félix Kir maintained morale by mixing white wine with crème de cassis. This imbued the paler vintage with the flavor of his country's beloved red and simultaneously created an early version of the famed cocktail Kir. A later two-part formulation combined Champagne with the crème mixture, creating the Kir Royale—an inspired innovation that has stood the test of time.

½ ounce crème de cassis or raspberry liqueur
3 to 4 ounces Champagne, chilled
Fresh black currants or raspberries, for garnish
Lemon twist, for garnish

Pour the crème de cassis into the serving glass.

Top with chilled Champagne.

Garnish with black currants and a lemon twist.

YIELD: 1 DRINK
RECOMMENDED GLASSWARE: COLLINS OR OTHER HIGHBALL
RECOMMENDED SERVING ICE: STANDARD, 1-INCH CUBES

THE RICKEY

As the eponymous owner of Rick's Café Americain, Rick Blaine is loath to drink with his patrons. But on the rare occasions that he does, his preference for bourbon is evident. And with its fortuitous nomenclature, *this* timeless, bourbon-based beverage could easily be among Rick's personal favorites. The Rickey takes a refreshing splash of bourbon and flavors it with simple syrup and lime juice before adding a touch of club soda. Light, refreshing, and evermore elegant, The Rickey is a classic choice to share with friends, colleagues, and of course, patrons . . . should you so desire.

2 ounces bourbon or gin
1 ounce lime juice
¼ ounce Simple Syrup (page 150) (optional)
4 to 6 ounces club soda or seltzer water, chilled
Lime wedge, for garnish

In the serving glass, stir together the bourbon, lime juice, and simple syrup (if using).

Add standard, cubed ice until the glass is two-thirds full.

Top with the chilled club soda.

Garnish with a lime wedge.

It's worth noting that during the course of the film, only Captain Renault risks calling Rick Blaine by the name "Ricky." Coincidentally, the purported inventor of the cocktail, Colonel Rickey, wasn't overly enthusiastic about the nickname himself. In an article titled "Not Proud of His Honors" published in 1901, in the *Wellsboro Gazette*, he is quoted as saying, "Only a few years ago, I was Col. Rickey of Missouri, the friend of senators, judges and statesmen and something of an authority on political matters and political movements [. . .] But am I ever spoken of for those reasons? I fear not. No, I am known to fame as the author of the 'Rickey,' and I have to be satisfied with that."

AMERICANO

The Italian officer, Captain Dorelli, often struggles to be heard over his companion's constant conversation. On observing this phenomenon, Captain Renault notes that, should Dorelli manage to get a word in, it would be "a major Italian victory!" Americano serves up a needling nod to the captain's fruitless pursuit. Bittersweet amaro and sweet vermouth are mixed with seltzer water to craft a stylish drink that would be right at home in Casablanca's cafés or the runways of Milan. An Italian victory all its own, Americano is sure to earn a hearty saluti . . . so long as there's a conversational lull, of course!

1 ounce sweet (red) vermouth
1 ounce Campari® or other red bittersweet amaro
2 to 3 ounces seltzer water or club soda
Lemon wedge or wheel, for garnish

Fill the serving glass two-thirds full with ice.

Add the sweet vermouth and amaro and give the drink a quick stir.

Top with seltzer water to fill the glass.

Garnish with a lemon wedge.

SUFFERING BASTARD

Created in 1942 as a hangover remedy for British soldiers, World War II's spiritous solution could just as aptly refer to a lovesick Rick Blaine. Crafted with brandy, gin, aromatic bitters, and ginger beer and heightened with a hint of lime juice, Suffering Bastard could just be the panacea for hangovers and heartbreak alike . . . even as the whole world is crumbling.

1 ounce gin

1 to 2 ounces bourbon or brandy

¼ ounce lime juice

1 or 2 dashes aromatic bitters

3 to 4 ounces ginger beer, chilled

Mint sprigs, for garnish

1 to 3 lime wedges or wheels, for garnish

Fill the serving glass two-thirds full with standard, cubed ice.

In a cocktail shaker filled with standard, cubed ice, add the gin, bourbon, lime juice, and bitters.

Shake for 10 to 15 seconds until well chilled.

Strain into the serving glass.

Top with ginger beer to fill the glass.

Garnish with mint sprigs and lime wedges.

SIDECAR

Originating at the end of World War I, the Sidecar is a classic cocktail whose star has only continued to rise. Made with cognac, orange liqueur, and a splash of sour lemon juice, this beverage has a variety of formulations—with the British and French versions serving different ratios of the same requisite ingredients. Pouring equal parts cognac, triple sec, and lemon juice, this recipe is decidedly French—just like quite a few of the patriots of Rick's Café Americain. Regardless of how one chooses to serve it, as time goes by the perpetually popular Sidecar is sure to remain a classic—just like *Casablanca* itself.

Corn syrup or water, for the rim (optional)
Granulated or raw sugar, for the rim (optional)
1 ounce cognac
1 ounce triple sec or other orange liqueur
1 ounce lemon juice
Orange or lemon twist, for garnish

To rim the serving glass: Pour the corn syrup into one small, shallow bowl and the sugar in another. Turn the serving glass upside down and dip the rim in the bowl of liquid. Then dip the moistened rim into the bowl of sugar, rotating the glass so that the sugar coats the entire edge.

Set aside while you prepare the drink.

In a cocktail shaker filled with standard ice, add the cognac, triple sec, and lemon juice.

Shake for 10 to 15 seconds until well chilled.

Strain into the serving glass.

Garnish with an orange twist.

NOTE: The traditional version of this cocktail is sweeter than most modern versions. Use 1½ ounces of cognac for a drier drink.

CLASSIC MARTINI

In the grand tradition of gin joints, Rick's Café Americain would no doubt have a litany of go-to martini recipes—among them, the Classic Martini. This timeless tipple mixes four parts gin to one part dry vermouth and tops the blend with a twist of lemon. Fresh, crisp, and exceedingly elegant, the Classic Martini would be right at home in all the gin joints in all the world . . . and especially so at Rick's.

½ ounce dry vermouth
2 ounces gin
Lemon twist, for garnish
Olive, for garnish

Chill the serving glass in the freezer for 10 to 15 minutes.

In a mixing glass filled with standard ice, add the dry vermouth and gin.

Stir in a counterclockwise motion for 20 to 25 seconds until well chilled.

Strain into the chilled serving glass.

Garnish with a lemon twist and olive.

ATLANTIC

Casablanca predominantly takes place in Morocco and France—two sites bordered by the Atlantic Ocean. Accordingly, the classic cocktail Atlantic makes for a titillating tribute. The beverage first appeared in 1937's *Café Royal Cocktail Book*, where its flavorful blend of triple sec, rum, gin, and a dash of absinthe made it an instant classic. A delightful drink packed with sweetly heady notes, the Atlantic makes for a memorable offering that can be served in any location—coastal or otherwise.

¾ ounce gin

¾ ounce rum

¾ ounce triple sec or other orange liqueur

Dash absinthe

Orange twist or orange peel, for garnish

If desired, chill the serving glass in the freezer for 10 to 15 minutes.

In a mixing glass filled with standard, cubed ice, add the gin, rum, triple sec, and absinthe.

Stir in a counterclockwise motion for 25 to 30 seconds until well chilled.

Strain into the serving glass using a strainer or large spoon.

Garnish with an orange twist.

AVIATION

Following its first appearance in 1916 in Hugo Ensslin's *Recipes for Mixed Drinks*, the Aviation dropped off many mixologists' radars—owing to the decades-long absence of one of its key ingredients. When the crème de violette liqueur returned to shelves, this flighty beverage enjoyed a resurgence—and has remained on bar menus ever since. Made from gin, maraschino liqueur, lemon juice, and that long-evasive crème, Aviation is an aptly named cocktail that would have made for the perfect, tarmac-adjacent, going-away drink for Rick and Ilsa to share. Bon voyage!

1½ ounces gin
½ ounce maraschino liqueur
½ ounce lemon juice
¼ ounce crème de violette
1 cocktail cherry, for garnish

In a cocktail shaker filled with standard ice, add the gin, maraschino liqueur, lemon juice, and crème de violette.

Shake for 10 to 15 seconds until well chilled.

Strain into the serving glass.

Garnish with a skewered cocktail cherry.

CHAMPS-ELYSEES

This famed French thoroughfare was the backdrop to a happier moment in time for Ilsa and Rick. When the audience is shown a glimpse of the former couple's past Parisian life, the pair are seen driving down the Champs-Elysees before the scene transitions to a rustic country road. Named after the first portion of that famed drive, this cocktail blends cognac, bitters, and Green Chartreuse with lemon juice and simple syrup. Sweet, tart, and headily strong, Champs-Elysees embodies the fortitude of the French resistance . . . and the sweetness of a pair of young lovers who will always have Paris.

1½ ounces cognac
½ ounce Green Chartreuse® or other green herbal liqueur
¾ ounce lemon juice
¼ ounce Simple Syrup (page 150)
2 dashes aromatic bitters
Lemon twist, for garnish

In a cocktail shaker filled with standard ice, add the cognac, Chartreuse, lemon juice, simple syrup, and bitters.

Shake for 10 to 15 seconds until well chilled.

Strain into the serving glass.

Garnish with a lemon twist.

This driving scene originally included dialogue to match the visual transition. Ilsa purportedly tells Rick that when she's with him, she doesn't notice whether they're driving in the city or on a country lane. But the line was cut before shooting.

BEE'S KNEES

It's no secret that Rick thought Ilsa was just the bee's knees. After all, the no-nonsense New Yorker's Scandinavian sweetheart held his attention from the moment he laid eyes on her in Paris until her fateful departure from the famed Moroccan airstrip. And this Prohibition-era cocktail—rumored to have first been crafted at the famed Café Parisian at the Ritz hotel—would have been the perfect offering for Rick to serve his star-crossed companion. Made from gin, lemon juice, and of course honey, Bee's Knees is a beguiling brew that's bound to elicit a screen-worthy swoon.

2 ounces gin
1 ounce Honey Syrup (page 150)
1 ounce lemon juice
Lemon twist, for garnish

In a cocktail shaker filled with standard ice, add the gin, honey syrup, and lemon juice.

Shake for 10 to 15 seconds until well chilled.

Strain into the serving glass.

Garnish with a lemon twist.

"I didn't do anything I've never done before, but when the camera moves in on that Bergman face, and she's saying she loves you, it would make anybody feel romantic."
—Humphrey Bogart, *Casablanca: Ultimate Collector's Edition*

BETWEEN THE SHEETS

There's plenty that goes unsaid between Rick and Ilsa when she first walks into his bar in Casablanca. And plenty that went unseen during films of their time, thanks to the watchful eye of the Production Code Administration (PCA)—whose strict guidelines prohibited films from featuring anything considered to be overtly risqué. With its intoxicating blend of cognac, rum, and triple sec, Between the Sheets serves as a nod to the slightly suggestive. This pre-Prohibition cocktail's popularity has stood the test of time . . . and outlived the PCA's once-stringent restrictions. For those looking to flaunt the rules, consider replacing the recommended triple sec with Grand Marnier for a more complex drink.

1 ounce gold rum

1 ounce cognac

1 ounce triple sec

¼ ounce lemon juice

Lemon twist, for garnish

In a cocktail shaker filled with standard ice, add the rum, cognac, triple sec, and lemon juice.

Shake for 10 to 15 seconds until well chilled.

Strain into the serving glass.

Garnish with a lemon twist.

The team behind *Casablanca* were very aware of the PCA and worked hard to avoid notice. This is why viewers never see a bed in Rick's apartment. The filmmakers did, however, include a few scandalous inferences from Captain Renault's corrupt visa surcharge to the use of a dissolve transition that hinted at Rick and Ilsa's romantic reconciliation.

NEW YORK SOUR

When Major Strasser speculates about the future presence of Nazi forces in Rick's hometown, Rick replies, "Well, there are certain sections of New York, Major, that I wouldn't advise you to try and invade." Like Rick's beloved New Yorkers, the iconic New York Sour is a force to be reckoned with. Not only does it serve as a tasty tribute to Rick's American origins, but it packs a prolific punch, too. Made from red wine, lemon juice, and either whiskey or bourbon, this is one beverage that's bound to make any expatriate nostalgic . . . especially one from the City of Dreams.

2 ounces rye whiskey or bourbon

1 ounce lemon juice

¾ ounce Simple Syrup (page 150)

1 egg white or 2 tablespoons aquafaba (optional)

½ ounce dry red wine

Lemon or orange zest, for garnish

Cocktail cherry, for garnish

In a cocktail shaker, combine the whiskey, lemon juice, simple syrup, and egg white (if using).

Shake vigorously for 25 to 30 seconds until foamy.

Fill the shaker with standard, cubed ice.

Shake for another 10 to 15 seconds until well chilled.

Strain into a serving glass filled two-thirds full with standard ice or one large ice cube.

Float the red wine over the drink by holding a spoon above the surface of the drink and slowly pouring the red wine onto the spoon, letting the wine overflow and settle on top of the drink.

The wine should settle under the foam created by the egg white, if used, but above the rest of the cocktail. This creates two or three distinct layers.

Top with lemon or orange zest, plus a cocktail cherry for garnish.

Major Strasser was played by Conrad Veidt—a German actor who fled the Third Reich after marrying a Jewish woman.

BLOOD AND SAND

Blood and Sand is a cocktail that would be right at home in Casablanca's desert locale. Well loved for its simultaneously sweet and smoky seasonings, it blends scotch, cherry liqueur, sweet vermouth, and a shot of Morocco's signature orange flavoring. If the classic approach seems a bit sweet for modern tastes, feel free to bump up the scotch to 1½ ounces for a dryer cocktail. Either approach to Blood and Sand will be the hit of any cocktail party.

¾ ounce scotch
¾ ounce sweet (red) vermouth
¾ ounce cherry liqueur
¾ ounce orange juice
Orange twist or orange wheel, for garnish

In a cocktail shaker filled with standard ice, add the scotch, sweet vermouth, cherry liqueur, and orange juice.

Shake for 10 to 15 seconds until well chilled.

Strain into the serving glass.

Garnish with an orange twist.

OPENING
BETS

APERITIFS &
HAPPY HOUR DRINKS

The beginning of a new game is marked by a fresh wager—with participants assessing their odds and laying out their opening bets. Likewise, these "Aperitifs & Happy Hour Drinks" make for their own fine start to a fun-filled evening. With recipes inspired by the setting, the characters, and iconic quotes, drinks in this chapter include Vultures Everywhere! (page 48) and The Germans Wore Grey(hound) (page 45). Fresh, thematic, and thoughtfully crafted, these "Opening Bets" are sure to pay off—no matter when they're served.

GIN JOINT JAUNT

Of all the gin joints in all the towns in all the world, Ilsa had to walk into Rick's. And there's no better way to honor her fortuitous arrival than with a Moroccan twist on a dirty martini. Playing off Bogart's famous line, this beverage combines gin and vermouth with a splash of lemon brine and adds in a drop of orange blossom—flavored water—giving this sumptuous, cinematic beverage a North African note. Garnished with lemon peel and classic martini olives, Gin Joint Jaunt will evoke nostalgic thoughts of a time gone by.

2½ ounces gin

½ ounce dry vermouth

½ ounce brine from preserved lemons

1 or 2 drops orange blossom water

1 preserved lemon wheel, for garnish

1 or 2 olives, for garnish

If desired, put the serving glass in the freezer for 10 to 15 minutes.

In a mixing glass filled with standard ice, add the gin, dry vermouth, preserved lemon brine, and orange blossom water.

Stir counterclockwise for 20 to 25 seconds until well chilled.

Strain into the serving glass using a strainer or a large spoon.

Skewer together the preserved lemon wheel and olives to garnish.

The first reader's report of *Everybody Comes to Rick's*, the play that would eventually be transformed into *Casablanca*, described Rick's bar as "[S]mart, sophisticated, luxurious . . ."

THE FRENCH DEFENSE

When viewers first see Rick, the lovesick proprietor sits before a chessboard that's been set up for the opening gambit, The French Defense. This potent cocktail serves as a tribute to Rick's barside strategy . . . and Humphrey Bogart's real-life love of chess. Made from scotch and absinthe rinse and flavored with coffee liqueur and gentian liqueur, this high-ABV lowball is a strategic opener that's bound to bring about a memorable evening. Checkmate!

2 ounces scotch

1 ounce coffee liqueur

½ ounce gentian liqueur or génépy liqueur

3 or 4 dashes black walnut bitters

½ ounce absinthe or pastis, to rinse

Orange wheel or slice, for garnish

Brown sugar, to brûlée (optional)

SPECIAL TOOL:

Kitchen torch or cast-iron skillet (optional)

Chill the serving glass in the freezer for 10 to 15 minutes.

In a mixing glass filled with standard ice, add the scotch, coffee liqueur, gentian liqueur, and bitters. Use a spoon to stir in a counterclockwise motion for 20 to 25 seconds until well chilled.

Take the chilled serving glass out of the freezer and pour in the absinthe. Swirl the absinthe around the glass, then pour it out. Or drink it, if you're into that.

Using a strainer or a large spoon, strain the contents of the mixing glass into the serving glass.

Add one large ice cube or ice sphere, if using.

If desired, brûlée or blacken the orange wheel or slice. Begin by sprinkling the orange with brown sugar to coat both sides. Use a kitchen torch and some metal tongs to blacken the orange. Hold the orange wheel with the tongs and apply the fire directly to the orange until blackened on the outside. If you don't have a kitchen torch, heat a cast-iron skillet over medium heat. Sear the orange wheel until dark brown and caramelized, 1 to 2 minutes per side. Set aside.

Garnish the drink with the burnt orange wheel.

THE FAMED WATERS OF CASABLANCA

RICK: I came to Casablanca for the waters.
RENAULT: The waters? What waters? We're in the desert.
RICK: I was misinformed.

When Captain Renault asks Rick why he originally came to Casablanca, the proprietor offers one of his signature, dry responses. Although the North African desert is, in fact, void of healing waters—this Moroccan-inspired mojito offers an inspiring alternative. The Famed Waters of Casablanca seasons the traditional rum, mint, and lime juice concoction with a heady cardamom-rose syrup. Light, crisp, and decidedly delicious, this beverage is bound to have travelers feeling refreshed!

10 to 12 mint leaves

2 ounces mahia, pisco, or light rum

1 ounce lime juice

1 or 2 drops Bartender's Saline (page 152)

½ ounce Cardamom-Rose Syrup (page 152)

2 to 3 ounces sparkling mineral water

1 lime wheel, for garnish

Mint sprig, for garnish

In a cocktail shaker, gently muddle the mint using a muddler or the handle of a wooden spoon just until the mint is slightly bruised and is fragrant, then fill the cocktail shaker with standard ice.

Add the mahia, lime juice, saline, and cardamom-rose syrup to the shaker.

Shake for 10 to 15 seconds until well chilled.

Strain into a serving glass filled two-thirds full with standard ice.

Top with sparkling mineral water.

Garnish with a lime wheel and mint sprig.

Neither Claude Rains nor Humphrey Bogart ever visited those famed waters. The only cast member to see the real-life city of Casablanca was Dooley Wilson, who played the pianist, Sam.

THE CUT-RATE PARASITE

Italian refugee Guillermo Ugarte is in the business of selling papers. He procures the exit visas his customers need to flee Casablanca, undercutting the unscrupulously high-priced Captain Renault to secure a solid share of the growing wartime market. Though Rick has no objection to Signor Ugarte's practices, he remains wary of the man's methods. In Rick's words, "I don't mind a parasite, I object to a cut-rate one." This drink offers a cheeky nod to Ugarte's wayward ways. Apricot brandy, Aperol, and lemon are topped with prosecco to create a sparkling, bittersweet highball. A top-tier cocktail, The Cut-Rate Parasite is sure to be the hit of any party—whether served freely or "for a price."

1½ ounces plum or apricot brandy

1½ ounces Aperol®

½ ounce lemon juice

2 or 3 drops orange or peach bitters

2 to 3 ounces prosecco, chilled

1 or 3 orange slices or orange wheels, for garnish

1 rosemary sprig, for garnish

In a cocktail shaker filled with ice, add the apricot brandy, Aperol, lemon juice, and bitters.

Shake for 10 to 15 seconds until well chilled.

Strain into a serving glass filled two-thirds full with ice.

Top with prosecco.

Garnish with orange wheels and a rosemary sprig.

Film legend Peter Lorre, who played Signor Ugarte in the film, was himself a Hungarian-Jewish refugee during World War II. Born László Löwenstein, Lorre fled to Paris and then London before arriving in the United States. Though he went on to build a career playing less-than-savory characters, Lorre was known for his generosity and lightheartedness. A practical jokester on the set of Casablanca, he liked to use an eye dropper to put out director Michael Curtiz's cigarette when he wasn't looking.

THE GERMANS WORE GREY(HOUND)

Rick remembers every detail of the last time he saw Ilsa. It was the day the Germans marched into Paris—one in which "the Germans wore grey, [Ilsa] wore blue." Such a memorable moment is perfectly encapsulated in this bittersweet beverage. The Germans Wore Grey(hound) takes the traditional greyhound cocktail and turns it on its head by adding German lager, grapefruit juice, and a sweet-and-salty rim. Tangy, tart, and with just a hint of bitterness, The Germans Wore Grey(hound) is best served with a side of melancholy. Round up the usual suspects!

Honey, for the rim

Gray sea salt, for the rim

1½ ounces gin

3 to 4 ounces grapefruit juice

2 or 3 drops Bartender's Saline (page 152)

¼ ounce Honey Syrup (page 150)

2 to 3 ounces hefeweizen or Kölsch

1 or 2 grapefruit slices, for garnish

Rim the glass with honey and sea salt.

In a cocktail shaker filled with standard ice, add the gin, grapefruit juice, saline, and honey syrup.

Shake for 10 to 15 seconds until well chilled.

Strain into a serving glass filled two-thirds full with ice.

Top with the hefeweizen.

Garnish with grapefruit slices.

A GARDEN WATERED WITH CHAMPAGNE

While preparing to flee Paris, Rick and Ilsa share one last drink at La Belle Aurore. There, the owner, Henri, encourages the pair to finish their bottle of Champagne . . . and then three more because he's vowed to water his garden with Champagne before letting the Germans drink any of it! In honor of Henri's pledge, A Garden Watered with Champagne blends crème de violette, lavender syrup, and rose water to create a floral Champagne cocktail worthy of a fiercely determined Frenchman. Santé!

¼ ounce crème de violette or parfait amour
¼ ounce elderflower liqueur
¼ ounce Lavender Syrup (page 151)
1 or 2 drops rose water or orange blossom water (optional)
3 to 4 ounces Champagne, chilled
Edible flowers, such as violets or lavender, for garnish
Fragrant herbs, such as thyme or rosemary, for garnish

If preferred, chill the serving glass in the freezer for 10 to 15 minutes.

In a cocktail shaker filled with standard ice, add the crème de violette, elderflower liqueur, lavender syrup and rose water (if using).

Shake for 10 to 15 seconds until well chilled.

Strain into the serving glass.

Top with chilled Champagne.

Garnish with edible flowers and fragrant herbs.

VULTURES EVERYWHERE!

As he picked their pockets, *Casablanca*'s brazen thief Ugarte cautioned his marks with a very specific plea: "I beg of you Monsieur, watch yourself. Be on guard. This place is full of vultures—vultures everywhere!" Such potent words deserve an equally memorable drink, and Vultures Everywhere! is nothing if not unforgettable. Rhum agricole and aromatic bitters are enhanced by two of Morocco's signature flavors—fig jam and blood orange. Sweet and light and serving up an unexpected twist, Vultures Everywhere! will have guests *on guard* as they beg for another round.

2 ounces rhum agricole or gold rum

1 tablespoon fig jam

2 ounces blood orange juice

1 or 2 drops Bartender's Saline (page 152)

2 or 3 drops aromatic bitters

3 to 4 ounces club soda, chilled

1 blood orange wheel or sliced fig, for garnish

In a cocktail shaker filled with ice, add the rum, fig jam, blood orange juice, saline, and bitters.

Shake for 10 to 15 seconds until well chilled.

Strain into a tall serving glass.

Fill the glass two-thirds full with ice.

Top with chilled club soda.

Garnish with a blood orange wheel.

GERMAN 77

On Rick's final day in Paris, Ilsa is startled by the sound of blasting shots. She asks whether the noise is cannon fire or her own heart pounding, and Rick relays that the shots are coming from the new German 77—a 77mm field artillery gun. In a twist on the French 75, this German 77 takes the established recipe and replaces the gin with a cherry-flavored German liqueur. The Germans may have outlawed miracles in *Casablanca* . . . but even they wouldn't object to sharing this brilliantly blended brew!

1½ ounces kirsch or other cherry brandy

¾ ounce lemon juice

½ ounce Orgeat (page 151) or Simple Syrup (page 150)

2 to 3 ounces Champagne, chilled

Cocktail cherry, for garnish

Lemon twist, for garnish

If desired, chill the serving glass in the freezer for 10 to 15 minutes.

In a cocktail shaker filled with standard ice, add the kirsch, lemon juice, and orgeat.

Shake for 10 to 15 seconds until well chilled.

Strain into the serving glass, with or without ice, depending on your preference.

Top off with Champagne to fill the glass.

Garnish with a skewered cocktail cherry and lemon twist.

Before *Casablanca*, Bogart was more accustomed to blasting shots than sounding the beat of a lovestruck heart. At the time of his casting, he'd played a gaggle of gangsters but never a romantic lead. Accordingly, he told a journalist visiting the set, "I've always gotten out of my scrapes in front of the camera with a handy little black automatic. It's a lead pipe cinch. But this. Well, this leaves me a little baffled."

CZECHS AND BALANCES

Victor Laszlo is quick to remind Major Strasser that he's a proud Czechoslovakian—one who never has and never will accept the so-called privilege of being a subject of the German Reich. Czechs and Balances pays homage to Laszlo's heritage while noting the delicate balancing act the freedom fighter must perform in order to evade Casablanca's authorities. Here ginger beer, mint, lime, and honey syrup are mixed with a touch of the traditional Czech liqueur, Becherovka. A unique twist on the more commonly consumed mule, Czechs and Balances is a drink one can *always* serve proudly.

1½ ounces Becherovka®

¼ ounce Honey Syrup (page 150)

1 ounce lime juice

1 to 2 drops Bartender's Saline (page 152)

2 or 3 dashes orange or other aromatic bitters

4 to 5 ounces ginger beer, chilled

1 mint sprig, for garnish

1 to 3 lime wedges or wheels, for garnish

In a cocktail shaker filled with ice, add the Becherovka honey, syrup, lime juice, saline, and bitters.

Shake for 10 to 15 seconds until well chilled.

Strain into a copper mug filled two-thirds full with crushed ice.

Top with ginger beer to fill the glass.

Garnish with mint sprigs and lime wedges.

Casablanca's screenwriters employed their own form of checks and balances. As part of their process, each partner took responsibility for a different aspect of the story. Howard Koch focused on making sure the film delivered a clear moral message, Casey Robinson took charge of the romance, and Julius and Philip Epstein added the humor.

PLAY IT, SAM

Among the most well-known quotes in film history, the line "Play it, Sam" is uttered by both Ilsa and Rick. In pleading with the pianist to play the couple's song, "As Time Goes By," Ilsa gives herself permission to relive her Parisian romance—if only for a moment. And in demanding Sam reprise the song, seeing as he's already played it for Ilsa, Rick rips the bandage from his wounded heart . . . and forces himself to face his feelings head on. Play It, Sam reinterprets the theme of heartbreak—combining bittersweet gentian liqueur with génépy liqueur and adding in a dash of lemon juice to evoke the hazy yellowed hue of an old photograph or a long-ago memory. With a hint of salt, Play It, Sam is a drink to sip alongside fond rememberings of a time gone by.

Lemon juice, for the rim

Fleur de sel or other salt, for the rim

2 ounces gin

¾ ounce gentian liqueur

¾ ounce génépy liqueur or other yellow herbal liqueur

½ ounce lemon juice

¼ ounce falernum

2 or 3 drops Bartender's Saline (page 152)

Dehydrated lemon wheel, for garnish

To rim the serving glass: Pour the lemon juice into one of the small shallow bowls and put the fleur de sel into the other. Turn the serving glass upside down and dip the rim into the lemon juice. Next, dip the moistened rim of the glass into the bowl of fleur de sel, rotating to coat all the way around. Set the glass aside while you prepare the drink.

To make the drink: In a cocktail shaker filled with standard ice, add the gin, gentian liqueur, génépy liqueur, lemon juice, falernum, and saline.

Shake for 10 to 15 seconds until well chilled.

Strain into the serving glass.

Garnish with a dehydrated lemon wheel.

Though often misquoted as "Play it again, Sam," that combination of words was never spoken in the film! It was, however, a line in the 1946 Marx Brothers' film, *A Night in Casablanca*.

ONE IN, ONE OUT

Shortly after local police arrest Ugarte, Ilsa Lund walks into Rick's bar—a phenomenon the proprietor pragmatically describes as "one in, one out." And this bourbon-based beverage with the mischievous moniker blends its primary liquor with ginger beer before dropping in a shot of Calvados. It's an unexpectedly sweet twist on a normally biting blend, proving that in life—and in love—things don't always happen as planned. And that's the way it goes.

1 ounce bourbon or rye whiskey

3 or 4 dashes aromatic bitters

2 or 3 dashes citrus bitters

5 ounces ginger beer, chilled

1½ ounces Calvados or other apple brandy

1 to 3 lime wedges, for garnish

In a pint glass, combine the bourbon and bitters and top with the chilled ginger beer. The glass should be a little less than half full.

Pour the Calvados into a shot glass. If you'd like, chill the Calvados by shaking it for 10 to 15 seconds in a cocktail shaker filled with ice before straining it into the shot glass.

Holding the shot glass just above the ginger beer, drop it into the pint glass. The ginger beer should fizz for a few seconds.

Garnish with lime wedges.

Drink quickly or add some ice to sip and savor.

Though Rick Blaine and Guillermo Ugarte weren't exactly friends on-screen, Humphrey Bogart and Peter Lorre were steadfast drinking buddies on set. Famed cinematographer James Wong Howe, who occasionally joined the pair in their libations, said, "I couldn't keep up with them. They would steam out their hangovers and go straight to the bar across the street and start drinking again."

A WISE FOREIGN POLICY

Rick Blaine sticks his neck out for nobody—which, according to the self-serving Captain Renault, is "a wise foreign policy." This version of the Captain's famed line is meant for anyone who might be slow to pick a side or make their move . . . but who will eventually find their way. Made from sloe gin, club soda, and egg white, A Wise Foreign Policy is a gin fizz with a protein-packed punch—one designed to be enjoyed by *all* parties as they decide whether they'd like to put some skin in the game.

2 ounces sloe gin

½ ounce Honey Syrup (page 150)

1 ounce lemon juice

2 or 3 dashes aromatic bitters

1 egg white or 2 tablespoons aquafaba (optional)

2 to 3 ounces club soda

1 lemon wheel or slice, for garnish

In a cocktail shaker, combine the sloe gin, honey syrup, lemon juice, bitters, and egg white (if using).

Shake for 25 to 30 seconds until foamy.

Add standard ice to the cocktail shaker.

Shake for 10 to 15 seconds until well chilled.

Strain into the serving glass, shaking to get out as much of the foam as you can.

Top with club soda to fill the glass.

Garnish with a lemon wheel.

Playwright Murray Burnett was inspired to write *Everybody Comes to Rick's*, the source material for *Casablanca*, while honeymooning in Vienna in 1938. The newlyweds were there just as Austria voted to join the German Anschluss, which made departing the country more dangerous than entering had been. When they managed a safe return to New York, Murray reportedly told his collaborator, Joan Alison, "No one can remain neutral, God damn it, Joan. No one can remain neutral."

DESTINY TAKES A HAND

Before his arrest, Victor Laszlo reminds Rick that everyone has a destiny—be it for good or evil. As the freedom fighter is taken into custody, Rick wryly observes that it seems "destiny has taken a hand" . . . although he eventually puts his own thumb on the scale when he rescues Laszlo from his seemingly dire predicament. Destiny Takes a Hand is an imbibable intoxicant made from gentian and herbal liqueurs, red vermouth, creole bitters, and brandy. Perfectly paired with a side of subterfuge, this cocktail is both brazenly bold and quintessentially bittersweet—not unlike the fierce freedom fighter and the unwitting sentimentalist.

1 ounce brandy or bourbon
1 ounce gentian liqueur, French amer, or amaro
1 ounce sweet (red) vermouth
½ ounce Bénédictine®
3 or 4 dashes Peychaud's Bitters or other creole bitters
Orange peel, for garnish

In a mixing glass filled with ice, add the brandy, 1 ounce gentian liqueur, French amer, or amaro, sweet vermouth, Bénédictine, and bitters.

Stir in a counterclockwise motion for 20 to 25 seconds until well chilled.

Strain into the serving glass using a strainer or a large spoon, adding a large ice cube or sphere, if desired.

Garnish with an orange peel, giving it a good squeeze to release the oils into the drink.

FOUR OF A KIND

Rick's signature term of endearment, the iconic "Here's looking at you, kid," was spoken four times over the course of *Casablanca*, spanning the highs and lows of Rick and Ilsa's love story, from the early days of their Parisian romance to their bittersweet farewell on a Moroccan airstrip. And just like the famed line, Four of a Kind will surely become a classic in its own right. Here four elements—bourbon, triple sec, chilled Champagne, and aromatic bitters—quadruple the flavor. Topped with an orange twist and best served in a frosted glass, this libation will no doubt be welcome anytime it makes an appearance.

1½ ounces bourbon or brandy
1½ ounces triple sec or other orange liqueur
3 or 4 drops aromatic bitters
2 to 3 ounces Champagne, chilled
Orange twist, for garnish

If preferred, chill the serving glass in the freezer for 10 to 15 minutes.

In a cocktail shaker filled with standard ice, add the bourbon, triple sec, and bitters.

Shake for 10 to 15 seconds until well chilled.

Strain into the serving glass, with or without ice, depending on your preference.

Top off with Champagne to fill the glass.

Garnish with an orange twist.

While playing poker with her fellow cast members, Ingrid Bergman uttered the phrase, "Here's looking at you." Her costar overheard the words and thought they'd make a delightful addition to their upcoming scene. Bogart's improvised line went on to become a cinematic classic.

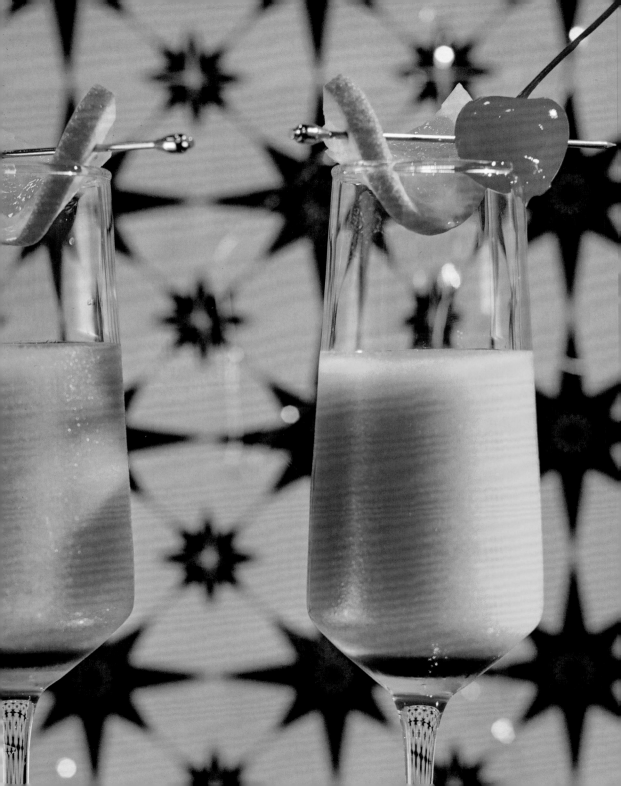

LA PARTIE CONTINUE

MID-EVENING PICK-ME-UPS

As the evening moves on, guests like those at Rick's Café may find themselves in need of a pick-me-up. Whether they're contending with letters of transit that might be up for grabs or the fallout of a sweet but short-lived love affair, these "Mid-Evening Pick-Me-Ups" may prove just the thing to propel any protagonists through the night. Offering fortifying flavors and cups full of courage, these recipes include Knock on Wood (page 66), which provides the ultimate music-inspired mood booster, and La Belle Aurore (page 79) for a chance to reminisce about a simpler time. With notes of romance and a hearty dose of bravery, the following tipples make a fine tribute to times gone by.

TRAIN TO MARSEILLE

When German forces occupied Rick and Ilsa's adopted city of Paris, the pair made plans to escape on a train bound for Marseille. Had Ilsa not discovered that her husband, Victor, was still alive, she and Rick would no doubt have toasted their new beginning with pastis—a beloved local aperitif. A nod to that ill-fated day, Train to Marseille combines pastis, vermouth, and orange bitters with tangy lemon juice and sweet orgeat. Tart, dry, and deliciously bittersweet, Train to Marseille captures the essence of that fateful day on the platform. Here's looking at you, kid.

1 ounce pastis

1 ounce dry vermouth

1 ounce lemon juice

1 or 2 drops Bartender's Saline (page 152)

½ ounce Orgeat (page 151)

2 or 3 dashes orange bitters

1 star anise pod, for garnish

In a cocktail shaker filled with standard ice, add the pastis, dry vermouth, lemon juice, saline, orgeat, and bitters.

Shake for 10 to 15 seconds until well chilled.

Strain into the serving glass.

Garnish with a star anise pod.

Because the script had yet to be completed when filming began, Ingrid Bergman was unsure whether her character was meant to be in love with her Parisian paramour or her erstwhile husband. When she asked the film's director, Michael Curtiz advised that she "play it in between" . . . resulting in her highly convincing, conflicted performance!

YIELD: 1 DRINK
RECOMMENDED GLASSWARE: ROCKS OR COUPE
RECOMMENDED SERVING ICE: LARGE ICE CUBE OR SPHERE (OPTIONAL)

KNOCK ON WOOD

While Rick speaks with Signor Ugarte about missing letters of transit, his popular pianist, Sam, is seen playing "Knock on Wood." This upbeat, participatory tune reflects Sam's own positive and steadfast nature. While he sings, his audience cheerfully raps cups atop tables in time to the music. Inspired by this unifying moment, Knock on Wood is an applewood-smoked ancestral lowball made from woody bitters. It's the perfect thing to serve any friend in need of a reminder to knuckle down and focus on what's in front of them.

1 ounce scotch

¾ ounce Calvados

¾ ounce sweet (red) vermouth

½ ounce Bénédictine

2 or 3 dashes maple, pecan, or walnut bitters

Cocktail cherry, for garnish

Lemon peel, for garnish

SPECIAL TOOLS:

Flame-resistant surface, such as a pizza stone or baking sheet

Long-necked lighter

Applewood or other wood chunk

Rinse the serving glass with water but do not dry it. Chill the damp serving glass for 10 to 15 minutes in the freezer.

Place the pizza stone or baking sheet on your work surface.

Use a long-necked lighter to light the applewood chunk and place it on the flame-resistant surface. You can also light the lemon peel, if you'd like.

Remove the chilled serving glass from the freezer and place it upside down over the wood chunk, let the glass smoke while you prepare the drink.

In a mixing glass filled with ice, add the scotch, Calvados, sweet vermouth, Bénédictine, and bitters.

Stir in a counterclockwise motion until well chilled.

Turn the serving glass right side up (do not rinse). Strain the drink into the smoked serving glass using a strainer or large spoon. Add a large ice cube or sphere, if desired.

Garnish with a cocktail cherry and lemon peel.

THE SECOND FRONT

A consummate consumer at Rick's Café Americain, Yvonne is also the proprietor's former paramour. She attempts to make Rick jealous by drinking with other men—be they French or German in their allegiance. Aware that Yvonne's determination makes her a formidable foe, Captain Renault wonders if, "[i]n her own way, she may constitute an entire second front." Made from crème de noyaux, cognac, and lemon juice, Yvonne's namesake drink is simultaneously strong and slightly sharp . . . a complex mix just like Yvonne herself.

1½ ounces crème de noyaux or other almond liqueur

¾ ounce cognac

1 ounce lemon juice

¼ ounce Simple Syrup (page 150)

1 or 2 drops Bartender's Saline (page 152)

1 egg white or 2 tablespoons aquafaba

Peychaud's Bitters or other creole bitters, for garnish

Cocktail cherry, for garnish

Lemon twist, for garnish

In a cocktail shaker, combine the crème de noyaux, cognac, lemon juice, simple syrup, saline, and egg white.

Shake for 20 to 25 seconds until very frothy.

Add standard ice to the cocktail shaker.

Shake for 10 to 15 seconds until well chilled.

Strain into the serving glass.

Add a few drops of cocktail bitters to the foam and lightly run a cocktail pick through the resulting droplets' centers to create little hearts, if desired.

Garnish with a skewered cocktail cherry and a lemon twist.

Madeleine Lebeau, who played Yvonne, was married to Marcel Dalio, who played the film's croupier, Emil. The pair shared a poignant connection with their on-screen characters, having fled from France ahead of the Nazi invasion. While en route to Chile, the duo was detained in Mexico—where they discovered that their visas were forgeries. After procuring temporary Canadian passports, Madeleine and Marcel were able to enter the United States.

LETTERS OF TRANSIT

Casablanca begins with the murder of two German officers . . . and the subsequent disappearance of two blank letters of transit the officers were rumored to have been carrying. These exit papers spark a series of events that play out over the course of the film—from Signor Ugarte's arrest to the self-sacrificing resolution of Rick and Ilsa's relationship. Letters of Transit is a smart combination of fruit-forward flavors named for the highly sought-after documents at the heart of this story. Rum and aromatic bitters are mixed with hints of pomegranate, ginger, and lime to create a recipe Rick would no doubt have kept in plain sight—no subterfuge needed.

¼ ounce crème de cassis or Grenadine (page 150)

1½ ounces spiced rum

¾ ounce pomegranate liqueur

¾ ounce ginger liqueur

¾ ounce lime juice

3 or 4 dashes aromatic bitters

1 or 2 candied ginger or fresh ginger slices, for garnish

1 to 2 teaspoons pomegranate arils, for garnish

1 mint sprig, for garnish

Pour the crème de cassis or Grenadine into the serving glass.

Fill the serving glass full with crushed ice.

In a cocktail shaker filled with standard ice, add the rum, pomegranate liqueur, ginger liqueur, and lime juice.

Shake for 10 to 15 seconds until well chilled.

Strain into the serving glass.

Give the drink a quick stir to blend the bottom layer and create a gradient effect.

Top with the bitters, which should float on top.

Garnish with candied ginger, pomegranate arils, and a mint sprig.

The letters of transit were the brainchild of Joan Alison—coauthor of the unproduced play on which *Casablanca* was based, *Everybody Comes to Rick's*. Her writing partner, Murray Burnett, expected the concept of inexpugnable exit visas to be challenged as too implausible, but it never was . . . and in fact, went on to become the lynchpin of one of the most iconic films in cinematic history.

TANGO DELLE ROSE

When Laszlo meets with his resistance contact, the agent signals his affiliation by lifting the stone on his ring and revealing the Cross of Lorraine—the symbol of a free France worn by Charles de Gaulle. While the two men meet, Mexican opera singer Corinna Mura performs a Spanish rendition of "Tango Delle Rose"—a song that doubles as the inspiration for this unique cocktail. Here muddled raspberries, rosewater bitters, and sherry are seasoned with lime juice and cardamom-rose syrup. Sweet, savory, and defiant, Tango Delle Rose is every bit as lively as its namesake dance . . . and song!

3 or 4 fresh raspberries
1 or 2 lime slices
2 ounces sherry
1 ounce guava juice
½ ounce lime juice
¾ ounce Cardamom-Rose Syrup (page 152)
1 or 2 drops rosewater or floral bitters (optional)
Rose petals, rosebud, or a small rose, for garnish
1 or 2 mint sprigs or lime wheels, for garnish
Fresh berries, for garnish

In the serving glass, gently muddle the raspberries and lime slices using a muddler or the handle of a wooden spoon.

Top with crushed ice to fill the glass.

In a cocktail shaker filled with standard ice, add the sherry, guava juice, lime juice, cardamom-rose syrup, and bitters.

Shake for 10 to 15 seconds until well chilled.

Strain into the serving glass.

Give the drink a quick stir.

Top with additional crushed ice.

Garnish with rose petals, mint sprigs, and berries. Serve with a straw.

LES JEUX SONT FAITS

French for "the chips are down," Les Jeux Sont Faits combines blackberry brandy and raspberry liqueur to craft a cocktail that matches the red-and-black color palate of a roulette wheel. With notes of grenadine and lime juice and a refreshingly foamy egg white, this beverage is just the thing to imbibe when the going gets tough . . . in love, life, or roulette.

1 ounce gin

1 ounce blackberry brandy

½ ounce raspberry liqueur

¼ ounce Grenadine (page 150)

1 ounce lime juice

1 or 2 drops Bartender's Saline (page 152)

1 egg white or 2 tablespoons aquafaba

Lime wheel, for garnish

Raspberry, for garnish

Blackberry, for garnish

In a cocktail shaker, combine the gin, brandy, liqueur, grenadine, lime juice, saline, and egg white.

Shake vigorously for 25 to 30 seconds until foamy.

Fill the shaker with standard ice.

Shake for another 10 to 15 seconds until well chilled.

Strain into the serving glass, shaking out as much foam as you can.

Skewer the lime wheel and berries for garnish.

THE BLUE PARROT

Signor Ferrari's drinking establishment and Casablanca's alternative to Rick's Café Americain is known for its exotic dancers, slightly shady clientele, and the signature macaw that serves as the Blue Parrot's mascot. This beverage takes inspiration from that cheerful avian charmer, combining dark rum and gentian liqueur with blue curaçao to recreate the macaw's blue and gold hues. Seasoned with fruit juice and a heady hint of cardamom, The Blue Parrot is worth its weight in carrying charges.

½ ounce blue curaçao

1½ ounces aged rum

½ ounce gentian liqueur

2 ounces pineapple juice

½ ounce lime juice

¼ ounce Cardamom-Rose Syrup (page 152) or falernum

Lime wheel, for garnish

Pineapple slice, for garnish

Pineapple leaves or mint sprigs, for garnish

Pour the blue curaçao into the serving glass, followed by crushed ice to fill the glass.

In a cocktail shaker filled with standard ice, add the rum, gentian liqueur, pineapple juice, lime juice, and cardamom-rose syrup.

Shake for 10 to 15 seconds until well chilled.

Strain into the serving glass and give it a quick stir.

Top with more crushed ice, if some has melted, until the glass is completely full and slightly overflowing.

Garnish with a lime wheel, pineapple slice, and pineapple leaves.

SHOCKED! (SHOCKED!)

Upon entering Rick's, Captain Renault is shocked—*shocked!*—to find out that gambling is going on in the café. (Amazingly, Renault manages to maintain a straight face when the bursar presents him with his winnings immediately following this pronouncement.) In a cheeky nod to Renault's feigned affront, Shocked! (SHOCKED!) brings together a range of zingy flavors—from peppercorn to lemon juice to Calvados. Blended with ginger liqueur and sweetened with honey syrup, this is one beverage that will leave anyone feeling like a winner—no gambling required.

Pink peppercorns

1½ ounces Calvados

½ ounce lemon juice

½ ounce ginger liqueur

½ ounce Honey Syrup (page 150)

Pinch ground cayenne or 2 or 3 drops spicy bitters

4 or 5 very thin apple slices or 1 center-cut apple slice from a small apple, for garnish

In a cocktail shaker, muddle the peppercorns using a muddler or the handle of a wooden spoon.

In the same cocktail shaker filled with ice, add the Calvados, lemon juice, ginger liqueur, honey syrup, and cayenne.

Shake for 10 to 15 seconds until well chilled.

Into the serving glass filled two-thirds full with standard ice, double strain the drink through a mesh strainer.

If using thin apple slices for garnish, create a fan with the apple slices and skewer them near the bottom half to hold them in place.

Garnish with the apple-center slice or the fanned apple slices and serve! SERVE!

LA BELLE AURORE

On their last day in Paris, Rick and Ilsa share a drink at La Belle Aurore—a charming establishment whose name translates to "the beautiful dawn." Although this moment was a bittersweet end for the dynamic duo, it marked a new beginning for Ilsa and Laszlo . . . one captured in a cocktail that mimics the hues of the early morning sky. And just like love itself, La Belle Aurore combines the sweet notes of elderflower liqueur and peach juice and liqueur with the bitter taste of gin. After all, a new dawn might mark the beginning of the end . . . but at least *Casablanca*'s ill-fated paramours will always have Paris.

¼ ounce crème de cassis or Grenadine (page 150)

1½ ounces gin

½ ounce peach liqueur

½ ounce elderflower liqueur

2 to 3 ounces peach juice

Orange wheel, for garnish

Cocktail cherry, for garnish

Pour the crème de cassis into the serving glass.

If using a Collins glass, fill the serving glass with standard ice.

In a cocktail shaker filled with standard ice, add the gin, peach liqueur, elderflower liqueur, and peach juice.

Shake for 10 to 15 seconds until well chilled.

Strain into the serving glass.

Stir the drink with a barspoon or straw to blend the layers a little.

Wrap the orange wheel around the cherry and skewer with the cocktail pick. Place in the glass to garnish.

According to the film's producer Hal B. Wallis, La Belle Aurore was the name of the real-life nightclub in the south of France that served as the inspiration for *Casablanca*'s source material, *Everybody Comes to Rick's*.

THE USUAL SUSPECTS

At the end of the film, Rick makes a risky decision: in order to ensure Victor and Ilsa's safe departure from Casablanca, he shoots the malevolent Major Heinrich Strasser . . . in plain sight of Captain Renault! As Rick awaits his imminent arrest, Renault surprises him by feigning ignorance of the attack and instructing Strasser's men to "round up the usual suspects." Renault's act of benevolence effectively lets Rick off the hook and signals a turning point in the relationship between the two men. The Usual Suspects immortalizes Renault's famous line by blending the usual suspects of cocktail making—citrusy juices, orange liqueur, simple syrup, and bitters. Blended with the liquor of the mixologist's choice, The Usual Suspects will be as unique as the bartender that blends it . . . and every bit as beautiful as an unexpected act of kindness.

2 ounces of one of *your* usual suspects:
gin, vodka, whiskey, or other base liquor of choice

1 ounce orange liqueur

½ ounce lemon or lime juice

½ ounce Simple Syrup (page 150)

2 or 3 dashes aromatic bitters

Citrus wheel, for garnish

In a cocktail shaker filled with ice, add the base liquor, orange liqueur, lemon juice, simple syrup, and bitters.

Shake for 10 to 15 seconds until well chilled.

If desired, fill the serving glass two-thirds full with ice.

Strain the cocktail into the serving glass.

Garnish with a citrus wheel.

A FRANC FOR YOUR THOUGHTS

ILSA: A franc for your thoughts.
RICK: In America they'd bring only a penny. I guess that's about all they're worth.
ILSA: I'm willing to be overcharged.

Ilsa's whimsical inquiry as to the nature of Rick's thoughts earns a wry observation on the value of conversion. But no matter the currency, A Franc for Your Thoughts is sure to be highly valued by those who succumb to its citrusy allure. Lillet, gin, and bitters are mixed with lemon and passion fruit juice and topped with the aptly named *Coin*-treau. With golden-hued liquors and marigold mixers chosen to match the sun, this beatific beverage will sparkle like a freshly shined franc.

Honey or corn syrup, for the rim
Coarse or granulated sugar, for the rim
2 ounces Lillet Blanc® or other aromatized white wine
1½ ounces gin
1 ounce passion fruit juice
½ ounce Cointreau® or other triple sec
¼ ounce lemon juice
1 to 3 dashes citrus bitters
Lemon coin, for garnish

To rim the serving glass: Put the honey in a small shallow bowl and the coarse sugar in another.

Turn the serving glass upside down and dip the rim (and sides, if desired) of the glass into the honey. Next, dip the moistened part of the glass into the bowl with the sugar, rotating the glass so that the sugar sticks all the way around the rim. Set the glass aside while you prepare the drink.

To make the drink: In a cocktail shaker filled with ice, add the Lillet Blanc, gin, passion fruit juice, triple sec, lemon juice, and bitters.

Shake for 15 to 20 seconds until well chilled and slightly foamy.

Strain into the serving glass.

Garnish with a lemon coin, squeezing it into the drink to release its oils, if desired.

A BEAUTIFUL FRIENDSHIP

After killing Major Strasser in order to ensure his friends' escape from Casablanca, Rick expects Captain Louis Renault to take him into custody. But when the opportunistic officer looks the other way, the duo embark on a new adventure together instead. A Beautiful Friendship is a sour that pays homage to Rick and Louis's newfound alliance, blending bourbon and orange liqueur in a pairing that's every bit as complementary as it is unexpected. Topped with a layer of foam reminiscent of the fog that hovers ominously above Casablanca's darkened airstrip in the final scene, this cocktail is a delightful drink that's sure to spark conversation . . . and maybe even a new friendship.

1½ ounces bourbon
¾ ounce Grand Marnier® or brandy-based orange liqueur
1 ounce lemon juice
½ ounce Simple Syrup (page 150)
2 or 3 drops Bartender's Saline (page 152)
1 egg white or 2 tablespoons aquafaba
Lemon wheel, for garnish
2 cocktail cherries, for garnish

In a cocktail shaker, combine the bourbon, Grand Marnier, lemon juice, simple syrup, saline, and egg white or aquafaba.

Shake vigorously for 25 to 30 seconds until foamy.

Add standard ice to the shaker.

Shake for another 10 to 15 seconds until well chilled.

Strain into the serving glass.

Skewer the lemon wheel and cherries to garnish.

Rick's parting words, "Louis, I think this is the beginning of a beautiful friendship," would go on to become one of the film's most famous quotes—and one of the most beloved in all of cinema. But the line wasn't included in the original script. Producer Hal B. Wallis asked Humphrey Bogart to come in a month after filming wrapped so the words could be dubbed in.

NO QUESTIONS

During the course of their whirlwind romance, Rick and Ilsa agree to live in the moment rather than parse each other's previous lives. But when Rick's curiosity about his heroine leads him to inquire about her past, she gently demurs by reminding Rick that they said "no questions." Just like the duo's determined pledge, No Questions is a mysterious cocktail that's delightful enough to elicit no inquiries. Here green liqueur, pineapple juice, and cardamom-rose syrup are blended with a liqueur derived from the beloved Norse elderberry, aquavit—a popular Scandinavian spirit. Light, fresh, and steeped in mystery, No Questions is a flavorful reminder to let sleeping stories lie.

1½ ounces aquavit

1 ounce Green Chartreuse or other green herbal liqueur

1 ounce pineapple juice

1 ounce Cardamom-Rose Syrup (page 152) or falernum

½ ounce lemon juice

6 thinly sliced cucumber ribbons, for garnish

1 to 3 dill or mint sprigs, for garnish

In a cocktail shaker filled with standard ice, add the aquavit, Green Chartreuse, pineapple juice, cardamom-rose syrup, and lemon juice.

Shake for 10 to 15 seconds until well chilled.

Strain into the serving glass.

Roll the cucumber slices into roses and skewer to garnish. To achieve this effect, stack two cucumber ribbons at a time and, starting at one end, roll the ribbons tightly into a spiral shape.

Repeat with the remaining ribbons and run the cocktail pick through their bases to secure.

Garnish the cocktail with the cucumber roses and dill.

LA MARSEILLAISE (VIVE LA FRANCE!)

To drown out the sound of the German forces belting "Die Wacht am Rhein," Rick's Allied patrons proudly belt the French national anthem, "La Marseillaise." With Laszlo leading the musical charge and even the mercurial Yvonne joining in, the ensuing sing-off shows the steadfast determination—and spirit of loyalty—kept alive by Rick's regular guests during the war. Like *Casablanca*'s patriotic performers, La Marseillaise is an uncompromisingly French cocktail. Made with an absinthe rinse and flavored with France's signature brandy, this is one beverage that will have everyone singing in delight. Vive la France!

½ ounce absinthe or pastis, to rinse the glass

2 ounces cognac

¾ ounce aromatized white wine

¾ ounce triple sec

¾ ounce lemon juice

½ ounce Lavender Syrup (page 151)

Fresh lavender or other fresh herbs such as rosemary or thyme, for garnish

1 lemon peel, for garnish

Chill the serving glass in the freezer for 10 to 15 minutes.

Take the chilled serving glass out of the freezer and pour in the absinthe. Swirl the absinthe around the glass, then pour it out. Or drink it, if you're into that.

In a cocktail shaker filled with ice, add the cognac, aromatized white wine, triple sec, lemon juice, and lavender syrup.

Shake for 10 to 15 seconds until well chilled.

Strain into the chilled, absinthe-washed serving glass.

Garnish with fresh lavender and a lemon peel.

Many of *Casablanca*'s actors were immigrants . . . with a significant portion having personally fled Nazi persecution. Accordingly, the performers' enthusiastic rendition of the French national anthem—and their ensuing tears—were heartwarmingly genuine.

LUCKY NUMBER 22

To win the funds to secure their exit visas, a young Bulgarian couple needs the roulette wheel to land on twenty-two—a result Rick successfully (and secretly!) secures. That fortuitous spin is commemorated with a namesake cocktail—one made with a Bulgarian plum brandy and Bénédictine. Topped off with aromatic bitters and seasoned with a touch of honey syrup, Lucky Number 22 carries just a hint of surreptitious sweetness—just like Rick's prickly proprietor.

1½ ounces rakia or plum brandy

½ ounce Bénédictine

¾ ounce lime juice

½ ounce Honey Syrup (page 150)

3 or 4 dashes plum bitters

2 cocktail cherries, for garnish

If desired, chill the serving glass in the freezer for 10 to 15 minutes.

In a cocktail shaker filled with ice, add the rakia, Bénédictine, lime juice, honey syrup, and bitters.

Shake for 10 to 15 seconds until well chilled.

Strain into the serving glass.

Garnish with two cocktail cherries on a skewer.

Before moving to Hollywood, Helmut Dantine, who played the Bulgarian gambler Jan Brandel, served as the leader of the anti-Nazi youth movement in Vienna. He was arrested during the Nazi annexation, and upon his release moved to Los Angeles . . . where he embarked on a successful acting career.

FINALES

NIGHTCAPS & DIGESTIFS

In roulette, a finale is a bet placed on all numbers that end on the same digit. And at Rick's Café Americain, the end of an evening is best marked by one last wager . . . or one final libation. After all, a nightcap or digestif is the perfect way to toast the end of one day and to ring in the start of something new. In *Casablanca*'s final scene, Rick sends Ilsa off on the next chapter of her adventures with Laszlo while embarking on his own new beginning—a beautiful friendship with Captain Renault. The recipes within this section pay homage to that bittersweet time of day (and phase of life!) when one thing ends and another begins. From the lyrically poignant As Thyme Goes By (page 93) to the emotionally charged Plane to Lisbon (page 108), these "Finales" will make for a fine ending to any festivities . . . cinematic or otherwise.

YIELD: 1 DRINK
RECOMMENDED GLASSWARE: OLD-FASHIONED OR ROCKS
RECOMMENDED SERVING ICE: LARGE ICE CUBE OR SPHERE (OPTIONAL)

AS THYME GOES BY

Throughout the film, both Rick and Ilsa ask Sam to play their love song, "As Time Goes By." It holds a special place in their hearts—and this take on an old-fashioned cocktail is a tribute to both that sentimental tune and old-fashioned romantics everywhere. Whiskey and aromatic bitters are mixed together and flavored with thyme and date syrup. Light, sweet, and romantically refreshing, As Thyme Goes By is an original twist on a timeless classic.

3 or 4 thyme sprigs

2 ounces bourbon or rye whiskey

⅓ ounce date syrup

2 or 3 dashes aromatic bitters

1 thyme sprig, for garnish

1 orange peel, for garnish

1 cocktail cherry, for garnish

In a mixing glass, gently muddle the thyme sprigs using a muddler or the handle of a wooden spoon, just enough that the thyme starts to become really fragrant as the oil releases.

Fill the mixing glass with standard ice, then add the bourbon, date syrup, and bitters.

Stir in a counterclockwise motion for 20 to 25 seconds until well chilled.

Strain into a serving glass using a strainer or large spoon. Add a large ice cube or sphere, if desired.

Garnish with a thyme sprig, orange peel, and a cocktail cherry. Give the orange peel a squeeze to release oils into the drink, if desired.

The song "As Time Goes By" was not created for *Casablanca*. It first appeared in the 1931 play *Everybody's Welcome*.

THE POOR CORRUPT OFFICIAL

When debating the amount to wager on the likelihood of Laszlo's arrest—a feat Captain Renault is convinced he'll accomplish—Rick proposes twenty francs. Renault counters with ten, claiming he is only "a poor, corrupt official." Modeled after a flip—an eggnog-style cocktail made with brandy, crème de cacao, and a whole egg—The Poor Corrupt Official is well suited to the opportunistic officer who frequently flips sides. Captain Renault's loyalties are always in flux, leaving his affiliation with whomever is treating him most favorably. But he'd no doubt pledge his allegiance to this flavorful nightcap . . . no matter which way the winds were blowing.

1½ ounces brandy or cognac
1 ounce dark crème de cacao
½ ounce walnut liqueur
1 whole egg
½ ounce cream (optional)
Pinch chocolate shavings, for garnish

In a cocktail shaker, combine the brandy, crème de cacao, walnut liqueur, egg, and cream (if using).

Shake for 30 to 40 seconds until creamy and foamy.

Add standard ice to the shaker.

Shake for 10 to 15 seconds until well chilled.

Strain into the serving glass, shaking out as much of the foam as you can.

Garnish with the chocolate shavings.

Claude Rains may have played the part of an official willing to take a "hands-off" approach to justice, but off-screen he was much more willing to get his hands dirty. In between takes on set, he could be found reading brochures on soybeans and fertilizer for his passion project: a farm in Pennsylvania.

CLEVER TACTICAL RETREAT

After attempting to confront Laszlo at Rick's, Major Strasser backs down in what Captain Renault decrees "a very clever tactical retreat." And just like the Major's strategic stand-down, this cocktail offers a brief respite from a frequently frustrating world. With dark rum, black tea, and warm spices, Clever Tactical Retreat is a sweet, heady libation that's sure to rejuvenate the senses. Cheers!

3 cups water

2 cinnamon sticks

4 whole allspice

4 cardamom pods, lightly crushed

4 whole cloves

2 star anise pods (optional)

Peel of 1 small orange, with no or minimal pith

2 black tea bags or 2 tablespoons loose black tea

1 tablespoon lemon juice

¾ cup orange-pineapple juice

3 to 4½ ounces dark or spiced rum

1 to 2 ounces orange curaçao or other brandy-based orange liqueur

2 or 3 fresh or dehydrated lemon wheels, for garnish

2 or 3 star anise pods or cinnamon sticks, for garnish

In a medium saucepan, combine the water, cinnamon sticks, allspice, cardamom, cloves, star anise pods (if using), and orange peel. Bring to a boil over medium heat.

Remove from the heat and add the tea bags. Let steep for 5 minutes.

Remove the whole spices and tea bags using a mesh strainer or slotted spoon, then stir in the lemon juice and orange-pineapple juice.

Put the saucepan back on the stove and heat over medium heat until simmering.

Add 1½ ounces of the rum and ½ ounce of orange curaçao to each serving mug, then top off each mug with the hot tea mixture.

Garnish with lemon wheels and star anise pods.

WE'LL ALWAYS HAVE PARIS

RICK: If that plane leaves the ground and you're not with him, you'll regret it. Maybe not today. Maybe not tomorrow, but soon and for the rest of your life.

ILSA: But what about us?

RICK: We'll always have Paris. We didn't have it, we lost it until you came to Casablanca.

Rick and Ilsa's parting words are among the film's most iconic. In urging Ilsa to remain with Victor Laszlo, Rick reminds her of her important role in her husband's work . . . and of the way she inspires him in his fight for the resistance. It's a conversation that's both a heart-wrenching warning and a sweet promise. We'll Always Have Paris is a cognac-based cocktail that harkens back to an idyllic and untouchable time in Rick's and Ilsa's memories. With notes of chocolate and a hint of berries, this rich, sweet cocktail serves up a swirl of romance in a glass.

2 ounces cognac

¾ ounce raspberry liqueur or crème de cassis

¼ ounce triple sec

1½ ounces pomegranate juice

1 to 3 dashes orange or chocolate bitters

1 to 3 raspberries, for garnish

In a cocktail shaker filled with standard ice, add the cognac, raspberry liqueur, triple sec, pomegranate juice, and bitters.

Shake for 10 to 15 seconds until well chilled.

Strain into the serving glass.

Garnish with skewered raspberries.

IT HAD TO BE YOU

The incomparable pianist, Sam, proves time and again that he can play love songs for the ages. His first such tune, "It Had to Be You," can be heard as the camera first pans in on Rick's Café Americain. A riff on Sam's delightful ode to love, It Had to Be You is a cheerful cocktail that's sure to please a crowd. Here gin, raspberry liqueur, and Champagne make a frivolous, floating base for a generous scoop of sorbet. With notes that are equal parts bitter and sweet, It Had to Be You embodies its namesake song . . . and feels as inevitable as a first love.

1 large scoop raspberry sorbet

¾ ounce gin

¾ ounce raspberry liqueur

2 or 3 drops chocolate bitters

2 to 3 ounces Champagne, chilled

1 mint sprig, for garnish

Put the scoop of raspberry sorbet into the serving glass.

In a cocktail shaker filled with ice, add the gin, raspberry liqueur, and bitters.

Shake for 10 to 15 seconds until well chilled.

Strain into the serving glass with the sorbet.

Top with Champagne to fill the glass.

Garnish with a mint sprig.

CARL'S EISKAFFEE

Rick's hardworking waiter, Carl, is a master of timing. When his boss is in his cups, Carl is quick to point out that Rick is getting to be his own best customer. And when Herr and Frau Leuchtag order brandy to toast of their imminent departure for America, Carl anticipates their invitation to join in the merriment—and arrives ready with a third glass to serve himself. Their toast takes place at the twilit hour of ten p.m.—and should the Leuchtags have inquired, Carl could have no doubt offered up a mental menu of energizing after-hours cocktails. Inspired by the litany of late-night libations consumed in Casablanca, Carl's Eiskaffee combines coffee, brandy, and a generous scoop of ice cream. It offers up a tasty tipple that makes for a delightful nightcap . . . in honor of the unflappable waiter who's always ready with amusing observations. Prost!

1 generous scoop vanilla ice cream

¾ ounce *good* brandy

¾ ounce dark crème de cacao

2 to 3 ounces cold-brew or strong iced coffee

2 or 3 dashes cherry or chocolate bitters (optional)

Pinch chocolate shavings, for garnish

1 chocolate-covered espresso bean or chocolate straw, for garnish

Put the scoop of ice cream into the serving glass.

In a cocktail shaker filled with ice, add the brandy, crème de cacao, coffee, and bitters (if using).

Shake for 10 to 15 seconds until well chilled.

Strain into the serving glass with the ice cream.

Garnish with the chocolate shavings and espresso bean.

S. Z. Sakall, who portrayed Carl, was a Hungarian cabaret actor who escaped to America during WWII. He was also known as "Cuddles"—a nickname bestowed upon him by Jack Warner, who insisted on including it in Sakall's screen billing.

PLANE TO LISBON

In its opening narration, *Casablanca* establishes the intended trajectory for many of the refugees that viewers would come to meet during the film: "With the coming of the Second World War, many eyes in imprisoned Europe turned hopefully, or desperately, toward the freedom of the Americas. Lisbon became the great embarkation point." In its final scene, the film makes good on a promise of sorts, as Ilsa and Laszlo board a plane bound for Lisbon. A cocktail with a keen sense of place, Plane to Lisbon makes a marvelous beverage to imbibe before embarking upon a bon voyage. Cognac, aromatic bitters, and port wine are combined with lemon juice and ginja—a sour cherry liqueur well-known in Lisbon. Sweet, tart, and rich, this is one flight that's bound to be smooth sailing.

1 ounce cognac

1 ounce ginja or maraschino liqueur

1 ounce lemon juice

¼ ounce Simple Syrup (page 150)

1 egg white or 2 tablespoons aquafaba

1 ounce port wine (optional)

2 or 3 dashes aromatic bitters, for garnish

In a cocktail shaker, combine the cognac, ginja, lemon juice, simple syrup, and egg white.

Shake vigorously for 25 to 30 seconds until foamy.

Fill the shaker with standard ice.

Shake for another 10 to 15 seconds until well chilled.

Strain into a serving glass filled two-thirds full with standard ice.

If you used maraschino liqueur, add a port wine float: Hold a spoon above the surface of the drink and slowly pour the port wine onto the spoon, letting the wine overflow and settle on top of the drink. It should settle under the foam but above the rest of the cocktail.

Garnish with the bitters.

In Murray Burnett and Joan Alison's play, *Everybody Comes to Rick's*, Lisbon was more than just a bookend to the story. In their theatrical version, Lisbon was meant to provide the original setting for the action. However, Julius J. Epstein, Philip G. Epstein, and Howard Koch's screenplay relocated the narrative to Casablanca.

THE WOW FINISH

Ilsa didn't keep count of the days she and Rick shared in Paris, but Rick certainly did. He recalled every one of them. As he told her, "Mostly, I remember the last one. The wow finish. A guy standing on a station platform in the rain with a comical look on his face because his insides had been kicked out." In a nod to that fateful final day, this cocktail offers a unique riff on the early 1900s classic, the Last Word. This version adds a Moroccan flair with cardamom-rose syrup, toasted almond bitters, and mint. Light, tart, and vivid as a memory that can't be shaken, The Wow Finish is a delightful drink that's perfect for sharing with someone special.

1 ounce gin

1 ounce Green Chartreuse or other green herbal liqueur

1 ounce lime juice

1 ounce Cardamom-Rose Syrup (page 152)

3 or 4 dashes toasted almond bitters

1 or 2 cocktail cherries, for garnish (optional)

1 lime twist or mint sprig, for garnish (optional)

If desired, chill the serving glass in the freezer for 10 to 15 minutes.

In a cocktail shaker filled with ice, add the gin, Green Chartreuse, lime juice, cardamom-rose syrup, and bitters.

Shake for 10 to 15 seconds until well chilled.

Strain into the serving glass.

Garnish with skewered cocktail cherries and lime twist, if desired.

Although the script was unfinished at the start of filming, with even Ingrid Bergman wondering which leading man was intended as her character's true love, the writers never drafted a version of the story in which Ilsa stayed with Rick. Instead, the screenwriters focused on coming up with a believable reason Ilsa would leave. In a note from Casey Robinson to Hal B. Wallis, he says, "The best thing I can come up with is that Rick clips her on the jaw and lets her husband carry her out."

JUE ZERO
NONALCOHOLIC DRINKS

Jue Zero, or roulette's zero game, offers its name to this chapter full of alcohol-free recipes. After all, the patrons of Rick's Café Americain were drawn in by more than drinks. For many, the company, the music, and the ambiance made all the difference. For such guests, this chapter includes drinks ranging from Reasonably Sober (page 119) to The Steadfast Pianist (page 121), each containing zero alcohol . . . but infinite amounts of flavor. No matter your audience, these tasty tipples should be a safe bet.

FRENCH 75 MOCKTAIL

There are times when one must keep one's wits fully in check. Perhaps a resistance mission requires alert attention, or a devious police captain must be imminently evaded. No matter one's plans, the alcohol-free French 75 Mocktail ensures one can remain sharp for whatever events the evening may bring. Made from juniper syrup, lemon juice, orange bitters, and sparkling water, this mocktail carries all the flavor of its alcohol-based counterpart. Vive la France!

JUNIPER SIMPLE SYRUP:

1 heaping tablespoon dried juniper berries, lightly crushed

½ cup water

½ cup demerara or turbinado sugar

½ teaspoon vanilla extract (optional)

MOCKTAIL:

1 ounce lemon juice

1 ounce juniper simple syrup

2 or 3 dashes orange bitters

4 to 5 ounces lemon-flavored sparkling water, chilled

Lemon twist, for garnish

To make the juniper simple syrup: In a small saucepan, bring the juniper berries and water to a boil over medium-high heat. Turn the heat to low and stir in the sugar until dissolved. Remove from the heat and let steep until cooled to room temperature.

Strain the juniper berries through a fine-mesh strainer and transfer to a sealable storage container, such as a glass jar. Stir in the vanilla, if using. You can use the syrup immediately, once cooled to room temperature, or seal it and store in the refrigerator until needed, for up to 1 month.

To make the mocktail: In a cocktail shaker filled with standard ice, add the lemon juice, juniper simple syrup, and bitters.

Shake for 10 to 15 seconds until well chilled.

Strain into the serving glass.

Top with sparkling water to fill the glass.

Garnish with a lemon twist.

AU REVOIR, VICHY WASSER!

As *Casablanca* comes to a close, Captain Renault tosses his Vichy water into the bin—a symbolic gesture that commemorates the end of his fealty to Vichy, France. He and Rick then walk into the fog, embarking on the beginning of their beautiful friendship. Au Revoir, Vichy Wasser! is a classic Mediterranean mint lemonade topped with an expected spritz of sparkling mineral water. Sweet, crisp, and utterly refreshing, this is one drink you won't want to bid adieu!

1 whole lemon, quartered

¼ cup fresh lemon juice

1 bunch fresh mint or about 20 to 30 fresh mint leaves

1 cup cold water

½ cup granulated sugar

1 teaspoon Bartender's Saline (page 152) (optional)

1 cup Vichy® sparkling mineral water or other volcanic water

2 to 4 mint sprigs, for garnish

2 to 4 lemon slices or wheels, for garnish

In a blender, combine the lemon quarters, lemon juice, mint leaves, cold water, and sugar. If you will not be using Vichy or another volcanic water with high salinity for the sparkling water, add about a teaspoon of saline, or just enough so it has a pleasant salinity to your palate.

Blend until all the lemon and mint pieces are puréed, 2 to 3 minutes.

Pour the contents of the blender through a fine-mesh strainer into a pitcher. Discard the pulp.

Divide the lemon-mint mixture into serving glasses filled with ice. Fill each glass anywhere from half to two-thirds full.

Top each glass with the sparkling mineral water (to taste).

Garnish with mint sprigs and lemon slices.

SIGNOR FERRARI'S SPICED ICED COFFEE

As the self-proclaimed leader of all illegal activities in Casablanca, Signor Ferrari is a highly influential man. His unscrupulous proclivities range from trading in illicit visas to attempting to purchase Rick's establishment and, barring that, to buy off its beloved pianist. Signor Ferrari's Spiced Iced Coffee serves as a nod to the Blue Parrot's underhanded owner and to the chilled coffee confection he once served to Ilsa. Creamy coffee is mixed with a home-brewed cardamom-rose syrup—adding a dash of Morocco's signature flavor. Strong, spicy, and packing a caffeinated punch, this is one frosty beverage to make a fortune off of—no black market required.

1 to 2 ounces heavy cream

1½ ounces Cardamom-Rose Syrup (page 152)

½ teaspoon vanilla extract

2 or 3 drops Bartender's Saline (page 152)

1½ cups cold-brew coffee or strong iced coffee

Small pinch ground cinnamon or lime zest, for garnish

1 mint sprig, for garnish

SPECIAL TOOL:

Milk frother (optional)

Use a milk frother to whip the cream until thickened but still pourable. Alternatively, pour the cold cream into a cocktail shaker and shake for 20 to 25 seconds.

In a serving glass, combine the cardamom-rose syrup, vanilla, and saline, then pour in the cold coffee. Give it a stir to mix.

Add enough ice cubes to the serving glass so that it's about two-thirds full, then pour the cream on top.

Sprinkle with ground cinnamon and garnish with the mint sprig.

The actor who played Signor Ferrari, Sydney Greenstreet, left his home in England at the age of nineteen to become a Ceylon tea planter. Drought forced him out of business and back to England, where he managed a brewery while taking acting lessons. He landed his first film role in *The Maltese Falcon* at age sixty-one—a masterpiece that also featured Humphrey Bogart and Peter Lorre. Greenstreet and Lorre would appear together in eight more films, including the legendary *Casablanca*.

MOROCCAN MINT TEA

Rick's Café Americain serves a veritable variety of beverages—from alcohol-laced cocktails to the signature dry drinks of the region. Moroccan Mint Tea pays homage to the latter, combining green tea with spearmint and sugar to create one of the town's more traditional drinks. Flavored with a splash of orange blossom water—a fragrant nod to the country's famed orange trees—this delightful, minty beverage can be served hot or over ice, making it the perfect pairing for just about any climate . . . from warm desert days to chilly North African nights.

3 tablespoons loose-leaf gunpowder green tea or 3 green tea bags

3 cups boiling-hot water

½ cup granulated sugar

2 cups fresh spearmint leaves

2 or 3 drops orange blossom water (optional)

2 to 4 mint sprigs, for garnish (optional)

SPECIAL TOOLS:

Teapot

Steeper (optional)

Put the tea in the teapot using a steeper if you are using loose-leaf tea. If using tea bags, add them directly to the pot.

Pour in 1 cup of the hot water. Cover and let steep for 3 minutes.

Add the remaining hot water, then stir in the sugar (to taste) and mint leaves. Cover and let steep for another 3 to 4 minutes.

If desired, stir in the orange blossom water and steep for another 1 to 2 minutes.

If serving hot, strain the tea into mugs and serve immediately. If serving cold, strain it into a separate container and let it come down to room temperature before serving it over ice in tall glasses.

Garnish with mint sprigs, if desired.

REASONABLY SOBER

RICK: Why did you come back? To tell me why you ran out on me at the railway station?
ILSA: Yes.
RICK: Well, you can tell me now. I'm reasonably sober.

After a long night at Rick's, a patron might find that they've imbibed a tad more than intended. Should that be the case, Reasonably Sober—a tantalizing twist on a common hangover cure— would be sure to set things right. Made from avocados, pistachio milk, dates, honey, and topped with nuts and chocolate candies, this nutty, verdant blend is a nod to modern-day Morocco's popular avocado smoothies.

Chocolate sauce, for drizzling
1 small ripe avocado, pitted and scooped
2 cups pistachio or almond milk
4 or 5 Medjool dates, pitted
1 tablespoon honey
1 cup ice
¼ teaspoon sea salt
1 to 2 teaspoons chopped pistachios, for garnish
1 to 2 teaspoons mini chocolate chips, for garnish
1 to 3 cookies or small candy bars of your choice

Drizzle chocolate sauce around the inside of the serving glass, either in a swirl pattern from the bottom to the top or in an up-and-down zigzag pattern.

In a blender, purée the avocado, pistachio milk, dates, honey, ice, and sea salt until silky smooth. Pour into the serving glass.

Garnish with chopped pistachios, mini chocolate chips, and cookies.

Enjoy with a thick straw or a spoon.

On the other end of the sobriety scale, when Humphrey Bogart returned home from a late night with friends in Las Vegas, his wife, Lauren Bacall, commented that they looked like "a rat pack." The group, which included Frank Sinatra, turned the phrase into their collective name: the Rat Pack.

THE STEADFAST PIANIST

Rick's perennially pleasant pianist is as loyal as they come. He's followed Rick from Paris to Marseille to Casablanca, lending a sympathetic ear whenever his boss looks to share his burdens. And even though Sam isn't interested in drinking with Rick, he's more than willing to stay up through the night to help him talk through his troubles. The Steadfast Pianist combines coffee, cocoa powder, bourbon vanilla extract, and almond bitters in a comforting ode to the friend who is willing to drive all night, go fishing, and *stay away* until the woman who broke Rick's heart is long gone.

1 ounce Orgeat (page 151)
½ teaspoon rum extract
½ teaspoon bourbon vanilla extract
3 or 4 dashes toasted almond bitters
1 cup strong, hot coffee or ½ cup each of espresso and hot water
1 ounce heavy whipping cream
Chocolate shavings or cocoa powder, for garnish

SPECIAL TOOL:
Milk frother (optional)

In the serving mug, combine the orgeat, rum extract, bourbon vanilla extract, and bitters and give it a quick stir.

Top with piping-hot coffee.

Use a milk frother to whip the cream until thickened but still pourable. Alternatively, pour the cold cream into a cocktail shaker and shake for 20 to 25 seconds.

Slowly pour or spoon the cream onto the drink (it should settle on top, creating two layers).

Garnish with chocolate shavings.

Dooley Wilson, who played Sam in Casablanca, was actually a drummer—not a pianist! Wilson only pretended to play the keys while Elliot Carpenter performed on another piano just off camera—where Wilson could watch and imitate his hand movements. When it came time to record the film's soundtrack, Jean Plummer played Sam's musical numbers, although Wilson sang his signature songs himself.

LA PARTAGE

HORS D'OEUVRES
& CANAPÉS

Whether Rick's patrons are enjoying a caviar service together or splitting their roulette wagers with the house as part of the rule of la partage, they've got one thing in common: sharing. This also happens to be the literal translation for la partage. However you intend to use the concept yourself, the ensuing "Hors D'oeuvres & Canapés"—from Couscous Stuffed Peppers (page 130) to Chèvre Stuffed Dates (page 140)—are meant to be shared . . . and are sure to result in *zero* leftovers. Bon appétit!

DIETARY CONSIDERATIONS

V: VEGETARIAN ◆ V*: EASILY MADE VEGETARIAN ◆
V+: VEGAN ◆ V+*: EASILY MADE VEGAN ◆ GF: GLUTEN FREE
GF*: EASILY MADE GLUTEN FREE

LEADING BANKER'S BANKET

Rick's Café Americain has one hard and fast rule: the proprietor does *not* drink with his patrons. When Amsterdam's second leading banker tries to get Rick to share a drink, he quickly learns that his status means nothing to the ex-pat . . . as Amsterdam's *leading* banker is currently working as the café's pastry chef! A cheeky nod to Rick's financially savvy employee (as well as a popular Dutch pastry!), Leading Banker's Blanket wraps a citrusy almond paste in a light layer of puff pastry. Sprinkled with almonds and dusted with confectioner's sugar, this dessert can be eaten alone or served with a nightcap . . . so long as one doesn't break Casablanca's curfew, of course!

DUTCH ALMOND PASTE:

2 cups almond meal

¾ cup granulated sugar

1 large egg, lightly beaten

1 teaspoon lemon or orange zest

½ teaspoon almond extract (optional)

½ teaspoon rose water (optional)

BANKET:

Two 10-by-10-inch sheets frozen, ready-rolled puff pastry

All-purpose flour, for dusting the work surface

1½ cups prepared Dutch Almond Paste or marzipan

1 large egg, lightly beaten, for washing

2 tablespoons sliced almonds

Confectioners' sugar, for dusting

To make the Dutch almond paste: In a medium mixing bowl, combine the almond meal, granulated sugar, egg, zest, almond extract (to taste), and rose water (to taste). Mix until a paste is formed, which should be about the same grainy texture as wet sand. Form this mixture into a ball or a log and wrap in plastic wrap. If it doesn't hold together, add water, a teaspoon at a time, just until it does. Set aside in the fridge for at least 1 hour or up to 3 days.

To make the banket: Thaw the two ready-rolled puff pastry sheets according to the package instructions. Preheat the oven to 375°F. Line a rimmed baking sheet with parchment paper.

Unfold the puff pastry sheets onto a lightly floured work surface.

Remove the Dutch almond paste from the refrigerator. Separate into two pieces and roll the pieces into two logs. Each log should be about 1½ inches wide and 1 inch shorter, lengthwise on each end, than the length of the puff pastry.

Place one almond paste log in the center of each sheet of puff pastry. Brush the sides of the pastries with the beaten-egg wash. Beginning with one pastry, first fold the shorter ends and then the longer ends over the almond paste log, wrapping tightly over the filling. Flip the pastry over so the seam is on the bottom. Repeat with the second pastry and log.

Transfer the filled pastries to the baking sheet with at least 1 inch of space in between them.

Brush both pastries generously with the egg wash. Sprinkle each pastry with the sliced almonds.

Bake on the middle rack for 25 to 30 minutes or until golden brown. Cover loosely with aluminum halfway through so the almonds don't burn. Once baked, let the banket cool on the baking sheet for 10 minutes, then transfer both to a cooling rack. Dust with confectioners' sugar.

Once they've cooled down enough to handle, slice both bankets into ½-inch pieces with a serrated knife.

CLASSIC CAVIAR SERVICE

During his initial conversations with Captain Louis Renault and proprietor Rick Blaine, Major Heinrich Strasser orders just one item of food: a tin of caviar. After delivering the dish, the waiter, Carl, tells Renault, "I have already given him the best, Monsieur. Knowing he is German and would take it anyway." In honor of this high-brow culinary craving, Caviar Service serves up a traditional caviar platter alongside an assortment of accoutrements—from crème fraîche to minced red onion to petite toasts. With a wide array of options—including hard-boiled egg whites *and* yolks—this fanciful offering is perfectly paired with a chilled glass of Champagne . . . just like the major ordered.

3 hard-boiled eggs

¼ cup minced red onion

¼ cup finely chopped fresh chives or dill

¼ cup crème fraîche or sour cream

1 to 2 ounces black caviar

1 lemon, cut into wedges (optional)

Blinis, petit toasts, crostini, and crackers, for serving

SPECIAL TOOLS:

Caviar serving set or large serving platter (optional)

5 or 6 small, ⅓-cup bowls

Medium shallow bowl

Nonmetallic serving spoon

Butter knife

Separate the hard-boiled egg yolks from the egg whites. Finely dice or grate both and put them into separate serving bowls.

Put the minced red onion, chives, and crème fraîche in separate, small serving bowls.

Fill a medium shallow bowl about one-third full of crushed ice. Open the caviar tin and place it on top of the crushed ice or transfer the caviar to a small serving bowl before putting that over the ice. Place a small spoon nearby for serving. A nonmetallic spoon is recommended, as metal might break the eggs.

Arrange the small bowls of toppings around the caviar bowl. Add the lemon wedges wherever looks best or in their own separate bowl.

Add your blinis, petit toasts, crostini, and crackers to a separate small serving plate or bowl.

To eat, spread some crème fraîche over your blini, mini-toast, crostini, or cracker. Add a very small amount of egg whites, egg yolks, red onion, and chives and top it all off with the caviar.

Squeeze with a bit of fresh lemon juice, if desired.

NOTE: It's likely that the caviar Strasser is eating is from a sturgeon from the Caspian Sea, which is considered traditional. The four major subtypes of sturgeon caviar are beluga, sterlet, osetra, and sevruga. But there are budget-friendly alternatives, including lumpfish roe, salmon roe, and whitefish roe. There are also a variety of vegan or "faux" caviars made from black seaweed, balsamic vinegar, black truffle, and even avocado.

Conrad Veidt, who played Major Strasser, said of the character, "I know this man well. He is the reason I gave up Germany many years ago. He is a man who turned fanatic and betrayed his friends, his homeland, and himself in the lust to be somebody and get something for nothing." Veidt went on to donate the money he earned playing Major Strasser to the British War Relief Society.

FIG AND OLIVE TAPENADE CROSTINI

With scenes set both in France and Morocco, *Casablanca* is a fusion of two vibrant locales. And this sweet and savory hors d'oeuvre is a unique fusion dish that borrows from the film's primary settings. Toasted crostini are topped with soft chèvre, chopped walnuts, and a homemade Moroccan-spiced tapenade, making Fig and Olive Tapenade Crostini a delightful dish that's bound to bring diners together—no matter their origins.

TAPENADE:

1 cup chopped fresh or dried figs

1 tablespoon olive oil

2 tablespoons balsamic vinegar

1 teaspoon Herbes de Provence (page 153), ground into powder

½ cup chopped kalamata olives

½ cup chopped pitted or stuffed green olives

2 cloves garlic, minced

Salt

Freshly ground black pepper

CROSTINI:

½ cup chopped walnuts or pistachios

1 loaf French bread

2 tablespoons olive oil, plus more for drizzling

8 ounces softened chèvre, Brie, or other soft cheese

Fresh thyme leaves, for garnish

Chopped parsley, for garnish

To make the tapenade: If you are using dried figs, put them and ½ cup of water in a small saucepan. Bring to a boil over medium heat and cook until the figs are tender and the liquid has reduced, 12 to 15 minutes. Skip this step if you are using fresh figs.

In a medium mixing bowl, mix together the figs, olive oil, balsamic vinegar, herbes de Provence, kalamata olives, green olives, and garlic. Season with the salt and pepper to taste. Cover and refrigerate for at least 2 hours, ideally overnight, to allow the flavors to meld.

To make the crostini: If desired, toast the walnuts in a dry skillet over medium heat for 2 to 5 minutes, stirring frequently to prevent burning. Toast just until fragrant and then immediately transfer the nuts to a plate and set aside.

Preheat the oven to 375°F. Line a standard baking sheet with parchment paper.

Slice the bread into ¼-inch-thick slices, place on the rimmed baking sheet, and drizzle or brush generously with olive oil. Bake the bread for 8 to 12 minutes or until toasty, flipping once halfway through. If you are using Brie or another similar melty cheese, place the brie on top of the toast slices after flipping.

To assemble the crostini, spread the toasted bread slices with cheese to taste, unless you melted cheese on top while in the oven. Place a heaping tablespoon of tapenade on top of each, more depending on the size of your crostini, then sprinkle with chopped nuts (toasted or otherwise). Drizzle with additional olive oil, if desired, then garnish with fresh herbs.

NOTE: If you opt for Brie as your soft cheese of choice, it is not vegetarian.

COUSCOUS STUFFED PEPPERS

The national dish of Morocco, couscous is both a mainstay and a local art form. Made from crushed durum wheat and rolled into small granules, large batches are traditionally prepared over the course of several days, then dried in the sun for several months. Couscous Stuffed Peppers offers a fresh take on this traditional meal, stuffing red bell peppers with Moroccan couscous and topping the treat with Greek yogurt and chopped cilantro. Light, fresh, and fantastically filling, Couscous Stuffed Peppers is a dish that's sure to please any crowd—from Casablanca to Paris!

⅓ cup sliced or slivered almonds

6 large bell peppers in a variety of colors

2 tablespoons olive oil, divided

2 tablespoons unsalted butter

1 shallot, chopped

3 garlic cloves, minced

1 tablespoon Ras El Hanout (page 153)

Salt

Freshly ground black pepper

2 cups chicken or vegetable broth

1 cup ultrafine (Moroccan-style) couscous

½ cup sultanas

⅓ cup canned chickpeas, drained (optional)

⅓ cup chopped fresh cilantro or flat-leaf parsley, plus more for garnish

1 to 2 tablespoons lemon juice

Labneh or plain Greek yogurt, for serving

Lemon wedges, for serving (optional)

If preferred, toast the almonds in a dry skillet over medium heat for 3 to 5 minutes, stirring frequently to prevent burning. Toast until fragrant and lightly browned, then immediately remove the skillet from the heat. Set aside.

Preheat the oven to 350°F. Line a baking sheet with parchment paper.

Cut each pepper in half lengthwise and remove the core and seeds. Place the peppers, open-side up, on the lined baking sheet. Drizzle the insides of each half with a small amount of olive oil and season with salt and pepper to taste.

Transfer the bell peppers to the oven and bake for 20 minutes.

Meanwhile, melt the butter in a Dutch oven or a large saucepan over medium-high heat. Add the shallot, garlic, ras el hanout, and salt and pepper to taste. Sauté until the onions are fragrant and softened, stirring occasionally, 4 to 5 minutes.

Pour the broth into the Dutch oven and increase the heat to medium-high. Bring to a boil. As soon as the liquid begins to boil, remove it from the heat. Stir in the couscous, cover, and let sit for 10 minutes.

Fluff up the couscous with a fork. Add the sultanas, chickpeas (if using), cilantro, lemon juice, olive oil, and almonds. Stir, adjusting the seasoning to taste as needed.

Remove the peppers from the oven. Evenly spoon the couscous mixture into each, then return to the oven for another 10 to 12 minutes, or until lightly browned on top.

Remove the peppers from the oven and spoon a dollop of labneh on each. Garnish with lemon wedges.

A HILL OF BEANS
(CRUNCHY SPICED CHICKPEAS)

Rick may not consider himself good at being noble, but as he urges Ilsa to leave with Laszlo, he reminds her that "the problems of three little people don't amount to a hill of beans in this crazy world." For those who'd like to test the theory, A Hill of Beans serves up a traditional Moroccan snack, coating chickpeas in spices and roasting the treats to crunchy perfection. Savory, salty, and poignantly crisp, this spicy side dish evokes Rick's conversational style . . . and *Casablanca*'s iconic locale.

Two 15-ounce cans chickpeas
2 tablespoons olive oil
1 tablespoon Ras El Hanout (page 153)
1 teaspoon smoked paprika
1 teaspoon garlic powder
1 teaspoon onion powder

1 tablespoon brown sugar
1 teaspoon lemon zest (optional)
¾ teaspoon salt

SPECIAL TOOL:
Air fryer (optional)

Preheat the oven to 350°F. Line a baking sheet with parchment paper.

Thoroughly rinse and drain the chickpeas. Place them on a paper towel and pat gently to dry.

Place another paper towel on top, then gently rub the chickpeas, removing as many of the chickpea skins as possible and discarding them. Do this for 10 to 15 seconds; it's not necessary to remove all the skins.

In a medium mixing bowl, mix the chickpeas olive oil, ras el hanout, smoked paprika, garlic powder, onion powder, brown sugar, lemon zest, and salt until well coated.

Pour the chickpeas onto the parchment-lined baking sheet and spread them into a single layer.

Bake for 30 to 35 minutes, or until crispy and completely dried, shaking the pan every 10 to 15 minutes or so to prevent burning. Alternatively, use an air fryer, cooking the chickpeas at 390°F for 15 minutes, shaking the basket once or twice to prevent burning.

Taste and adjust the seasoning to taste while still hot.

Allow to cool for at least 30 minutes before serving.

MERGUEZ BOULETTES

Drawing on influences from Morocco and France—both of which served as backdrops during transformational moments in Ilsa and Rick's love story—Merguez Boulettes serve up a decidedly multinational dish. Lamb or beef is rolled into balls, then breaded and fried to perfection. Heavily spiced and heartily seasoned, Merguez Boulettes are a savory snack to turn to in times of tribulation. As Rick explains, everybody in Casablanca has problems. But with the right comfort food, and the right companions, those problems might just work themselves out!

MERGUEZ BOULETTES:

1½ teaspoons cumin seeds

1 teaspoon coriander seeds

½ teaspoon fennel seeds

1 pound ground lamb or beef

1 to 2 teaspoons harissa paste

4 cloves garlic, minced

1 teaspoon salt

½ teaspoon smoked paprika

½ teaspoon cinnamon

1 large egg, lightly beaten

¾ cup plus 1 tablespoon panko breadcrumbs, divided

¼ cup chopped fresh cilantro, mint, or flat-leaf parsley

MINTED YOGURT SAUCE:

¾ cup labneh or plain Greek yogurt

½ cup chopped fresh mint leaves, packed

2 tablespoons preserved lemon juice (or regular lemon juice, salted)

2 cloves garlic, minced

Olive oil, for greasing

FOR SERVING:

Chopped fresh cilantro or mint, for garnish (optional)

Warm flatbread (optional)

SPECIAL TOOLS:

Kitchen gloves (optional)

Mini muffin tin

Bamboo skewers or toothpicks

To make the merguez boulettes: Toast the cumin, coriander, and fennel seeds in a dry skillet over medium-low heat until fragrant, 1 to 2 minutes. Use a mortar and pestle to grind the toasted spices to a powder.

In a large mixing bowl, combine the ground toasted spices, ground lamb, harissa paste (to taste), garlic, salt (to taste), paprika, cinnamon, egg, 1 tablespoon of breadcrumbs, and cilantro. Mix until thoroughly blended. Cover with plastic wrap and refrigerate for at least 1 hour, up to overnight.

To make the minted yogurt sauce: In a small bowl, stir to combine the labneh, mint leaves, lemon juice, and garlic cloves. Adjust the seasonings to taste. Place in the refrigerator until ready to serve, giving the flavors time to meld.

Preheat the oven to 400°F. Grease a muffin tin with olive oil.

Put the remaining nearly ¾ cup of breadcrumbs into a small bowl. Take the meat mixture out of the fridge and use your hands (put on kitchen gloves, if desired) to create golf ball–size meatballs. Roll each of the meatballs in the breadcrumbs and place each in individual muffin tin cups. Repeat until you have used all the meat mixture.

Bake until golden and cooked through, about 15 to 20 minutes.

Use toothpicks to skewer individual meatballs or bamboo skewers to hold two to four meatballs together. Arrange these on a platter. Garnish with fresh herbs (if using) and serve with the minted yogurt sauce on the side and warm flatbread (if using).

FETA CIGARS
WITH SPICED HONEY AND PISTACHIOS

Tobacco may not have been easy to come by during WWII, but just like exit visas—and other seemingly out-of-reach items—cigars found their way into Rick's Café Americain . . . where billows of smoke chased the bellows of song. Inspired by the patron's proclivities, these phyllo-wrapped, cigar-shaped pastries offer a tasty twist on that war-era past time. Feta cheese is drizzled with harissa-spiced honey, wrapped in dough, and topped with pistachios. Rich in protein and robust in flavor, Feta Cigars with Spiced Honey and Pistachios tantalize the taste buds and keep diners going through long nights of singing around a piano . . . or playing a rousing round of roulette!

¼ cup chopped pistachios

1 package frozen spring roll pastry, thawed

Neutral oil, such as peanut or vegetable oil, for frying

FILLING:

8 ounces feta cheese, crumbled

8 ounces grated mozzarella

2 large eggs, lightly beaten, divided

3 cloves garlic, minced

2 or 3 green onions, chopped

½ cup chopped fresh flat-leaf parsley, mint, or cilantro

SPICED HONEY:

¼ cup honey

1 teaspoon harissa paste

SPECIAL TOOL:

Kitchen thermometer

Toast the pistachios in a dry skillet over medium heat for 2 to 5 minutes, stirring frequently to prevent burning. Toast just until fragrant and then immediately transfer the nuts to a plate and set aside.

To make the filling: In a medium mixing bowl, mix the feta, mozzarella, one of the eggs, the garlic, green onions, and parsley.

On a clean surface, open up the thawed pastry sheets and take out a few at a time. Cover the rest with a damp towel to prevent them from drying out.

Unless otherwise directed by the package instructions for the spring roll pastry, lay out one of the sheets to form a diamond shape. Take a heaping tablespoon of the filling and form it into a 2-inch log by rolling it between your hands and then placing it in the bottom center of the pastry sheet. Brush the bottom tip of the sheet with the beaten egg, fold it over the filling, and roll once to ensure the filling is secure. Brush with the beaten egg and fold in the two sides, ensuring you create at least a 1-inch inward fold on each side so the filling won't leak out the sides when frying. It should look a bit like an envelope at this point. Finally, brush the exposed edges with the beaten egg and roll forward, tightly securing the roll. Repeat with new pastry sheets until all the filling has been used up.

In a cast-iron skillet or thick-bottomed pot, heat 2 inches of oil to 365°F. It's important that the oil is hot enough to fry the cigars before the cheese melts too much inside and leaks out. Fry the cigars in batches (do not overcrowd the skillet) for 1 to 2 minutes on each side until crisp and golden on both sides. Set the finished cigars aside on a paper towel–lined plate.

To make the spiced honey: First, loosen the honey by placing it, in the original bottle, inside a pot. Pour hot water (do not exceed 110°F) into the pot and allow the honey to sit in the hot water bath until it melts. Once the honey is runny, stir ¼ cup of honey and harissa paste (to taste) together in a small bowl until well combined.

Plate the cigars on the serving platter. Drizzle with the spiced honey and sprinkle with toasted pistachios. Serve immediately!

NOTE: Not all feta or mozzarella cheeses are vegetarian. Look for versions without animal rennet for a vegetarian option.

SMOKED SALMON TARTINES

A traditional French dish—and a classic in Norway, too!—these petite open-face sandwiches offer a taste of something special. Though Oslo's Ilsa and her New York–born, Parisian paramour would have known these delicacies by differing names, the pair would have been united in their love of the bite-size bread treats. Toasted dough is topped with an herbed cream cheese spread and served with cold-smoked salmon and an assortment of accoutrements. It's a light yet filling appetizer that's equally at home in the City of Lights or served beneath the Northern Lights that dance across Ilsa's homeland.

HERBED CREAM CHEESE SPREAD:

8 ounces cream cheese, softened

¼ cup chopped fresh cilantro

¼ cup chopped fresh chives

¼ cup chopped fresh flat-leaf parsley

1 teaspoon Ras El Hanout (page 153) (optional)

1 teaspoon finely ground Herbes de Provence (page 153)

½ teaspoon lemon zest or minced preserved lemon

Salt

Freshly ground black pepper

TARTINES:

1 shallot or ½ small red onion, very thinly sliced

1 tablespoon granulated sugar (optional)

Salt

Freshly ground black pepper

¼ cup lemon juice (optional)

1 tablespoon extra-virgin olive oil, plus more for drizzling

2 tablespoons capers, rinsed and patted very dry

8 slices crusty, flavorful bread

½ pound smoked salmon

Microgreens or chopped fresh herbs, for garnish

To make the herbed cream cheese spread: In a small mixing bowl, mix together the cream cheese, cilantro, chives, parsley, ras el hanout, herbes de Provence, lemon zest, and salt and pepper to taste until well combined. To use as soon as possible, set aside for 30 minutes at room temperature. If you won't be serving right away, prepare with enough time to set in the refrigerator for at least 2 hours or up to overnight.

To make the tartines: If desired, begin with a quick pickle of the shallot or onion. To do this, put the shallot or onion in a small nonreactive bowl and season with sugar, salt, and pepper. Cover with lemon juice (if using) and set aside for 30 to 60 minutes.

In a small skillet, heat the oil over medium-high heat. Fry the capers until crisp, 2 to 3 minutes.

Drain on paper towels.

Lightly toast the bread slices just until crisp.

Use a butter knife to spread the herbed cream cheese spread on each piece of toast to your taste.

Layer the smoked salmon evenly on each piece of toast.

Top with the sliced red onions, fried capers, and microgreens.

Drizzle with olive oil, then season with salt and pepper to taste.

CHÈVRE STUFFED DATES

A cornerstone of Moroccan cuisine, dates are used in everything from sweet desserts to savory dishes. Believed to have originated between Egypt and Mesopotamia circa 4000 BC, dates can be eaten alone or cooked into a meal. A decidedly more modern take on the millennia-old classic, Chèvre Stuffed Dates stuff the fabled fruit with a soft goat cheese, then top the treat with crushed walnuts, pomegranate arils, and herbs. Drizzled with a pomegranate-molasses glaze and sprinkled with spices, these dates are a dish that diners aren't likely to regret tasting—not today, not tomorrow, and not anytime soon . . .

GLAZE:

¼ cup pomegranate molasses

2 tablespoons honey

1 teaspoon orange zest

2 teaspoons Ras El Hanout (page 153)

Salt

Freshly ground black pepper

STUFFED DATES:

12 ounces or about 14 to 16 pitted Medjool dates

4 ounces plain or herbed chèvre

⅓ cup finely chopped pistachios or walnuts

3 tablespoons pomegranate arils

1 tablespoon chopped fresh herbs, for garnish

To make the glaze: In a small saucepan, heat the pomegranate molasses, honey, orange zest, ras el hanout, salt, and pepper over medium-high heat, stirring occasionally, until the glaze is a thick syrupy consistency, 10 to 15 minutes. Set aside.

To make the stuffed dates: Use a paring knife to slice the dates open lengthwise, taking care not to slice all the way through. Gently pull the dates open and fill each one with 1 to 2 teaspoons of chèvre.

Use a spoon to drizzle the glaze over the stuffed dates, then sprinkle with the pistachios and pomegranate arils.

Arrange the stuffed dates on a serving plate and garnish with fresh herbs.

NOTE: Some chèvre may contain animal byproducts. Look for versions not prepared with animal rennet if you'd like to keep this dish vegetarian.

ZAALOUK
WITH FLATBREAD AND CRUDITÉS

This classic Moroccan dip combines eggplant and tomatoes in a colorful relish that's brimming with flavor. Served over flatbread and paired with an assortment of French-style crudités, this vegetarian hors d'oeuvre lends an elegant air to any party . . . and will no doubt be the toast of *any* town!

ZAALOUK:
1 large eggplant, peeled and coarsely chopped

4 large tomatoes, blanched, peeled, and chopped

4 cloves garlic, minced

¼ cup chopped fresh cilantro, plus more for garnish

¼ cup chopped fresh flat-leaf parsley, plus more for garnish

1 tablespoon Ras El Hanout (page 153)

¼ cup extra-virgin olive oil

Salt

Freshly ground black pepper

1 teaspoon lemon juice (optional)

FOR SERVING:
Olive oil or chilie oil, for drizzling

Warm flatbread

Assorted olives

Assorted raw vegetables

Feta cheese cubes (optional)

SPECIAL TOOLS:
Potato masher (optional)

Shallow serving bowl

Serving platter

To prepare the zaalouk: In a deep skillet or medium saucepan, combine the eggplant, tomatoes, garlic, cilantro, parsley, ras el hanout, olive oil, and salt and pepper to taste. Cover and simmer over medium heat for 30 to 40 minutes, stirring occasionally.

Using a potato masher or a fork, crush and blend the tomatoes and eggplant. Taste and adjust the seasoning to taste, then add the lemon juice (if using).

Continue to cook for another 10 to 15 minutes, until the liquid has reduced enough so that the mixture will stay put when moved with a wooden spoon.

Transfer to a shallow serving bowl and drizzle with olive oil. Top with chopped fresh cilantro and parsley.

Serve on a platter with warm flatbread, an assortment of olives, raw veggies, and feta cheese (if using).

MA'AKOUDA (POTATO BEIGNETS)

Originating in Algiers, Ma'akouda make for a popular Moroccan street food. These spiced potato beignets offer an extra burst of flavor via the harissa dipping sauce. Hot, savory, and overflowing with savory seasonings, Ma'akouda are perfectly paired with strong cocktails and beautiful friendships.

HARISSA DIPPING SAUCE:

½ cup plain yogurt or mayonnaise

1½ tablespoons harissa paste

1 teaspoon smoked paprika

2 cloves garlic, minced,
or 1 teaspoon garlic powder

1 tablespoon lemon juice

½ teaspoon date syrup or honey (optional)

Salt

Freshly ground black pepper

1 to 2 tablespoons milk, plus more as
needed (optional)

MA'AKOUDA:

4 Yukon Gold potatoes, peeled and cut into
eighths

1 tablespoon salt, divided

2 tablespoons unsalted butter

1 shallot, finely chopped

4 cloves garlic, minced

1½ tablespoons Ras El Hanout (page 153)

1 teaspoon turmeric

¼ cup coarsely chopped fresh cilantro,
plus more for garnish

1 large egg, lightly beaten

½ cup all-purpose flour
(look for gluten-free versions, if desired), for
coating, plus more as needed

Oil, for frying

To make the harissa dipping sauce: In a small bowl, whisk together the yogurt, harissa paste (to taste), smoked paprika, garlic, lemon juice, date syrup (if using), salt, and pepper until well combined. It should be a smooth, creamy consistency. Thin it out with a bit of milk if the sauce is too thick for your taste. Adjust the seasonings to taste. Set aside in the refrigerator while you prepare the rest of the dish, or, if you won't be serving right away, up to overnight.

To make the ma'akouda: Put the potatoes in a large pot and add enough water to cover the potatoes by an inch, adding 2 teaspoons of salt to the water. Boil the potatoes over medium-high heat until softened enough to be pierced easily with a fork. Rinse the potatoes with cold water, then cover and let cool, covered, in the refrigerator for at least 2 hours or overnight.

In a medium skillet, melt the butter over medium-high heat. Add the shallot and sauté for 4 to 5 minutes until softened and lightly browned. Add the garlic and cook for another minute or two.

Set aside.

Using the large side of a cheese grater, grate the cold potatoes into a large mixing bowl. Stir in the shallot and garlic, the ras el hanout, turmeric, the remaining salt, and the cilantro. Adjust the seasonings to taste. Once it's to your liking, stir in the egg.

Put the flour in a shallow bowl. With damp hands, form the batter into round patties about 3 inches in diameter, then coat the patties in the flour. Repeat until you have used all the batter.

In a cast-iron skillet, heat ¼ inch of oil over high heat until sizzling hot. Test the oil by adding a small amount of batter; it should sizzle and bubble right away. Reduce the heat to medium and cook until the patties are golden brown and crispy on the outside and soft inside, 6 to 8 minutes per side.

Serve warm with the dipping sauce, garnished with more chopped cilantro, if desired.

VICHYSSOISE AMUSE BOUCHE

Vichyssoise—a chilled French soup—is made with potatoes, cream, and leeks—ingredients that could evoke the airy feel and flavor of the French countryside, even in the years encompassing World War II. Adapted for a cocktail hour filled with mixing and mingling, Vichyssoise Amuse Bouche serves this soup in small shot glasses that would no doubt be on hand at an establishment like Rick's Café Americain. Rich, cool, and flavorfully filling, this is one hors d'oeuvre that's guaranteed to amuse a crowd.

2 tablespoons unsalted butter

3 leeks, white and light green parts only, thinly sliced

2 large Yukon Gold potatoes, peeled and cut into 1-inch cubes

1 cup chicken or vegetable broth

¼ cup heavy cream

¼ cup crème fraîche, plus more for topping

½ teaspoon ground nutmeg

Salt

Freshly ground black pepper

Chives, chopped, for garnish

Croutons, for garnish (optional)

In a stockpot or Dutch oven, melt the butter over medium-low heat. Add the leeks and sweat, stirring occasionally, for 5 to 6 minutes.

Add the potatoes and cook for another minute or two.

Add the chicken or vegetable broth and bring to a boil over medium-high heat, then reduce the heat to low and simmer, covered, for about 30 minutes. The leeks and potatoes should be very soft.

Remove from the heat and allow to cool for 10 to 15 minutes.

Transfer the soup to a blender, making sure the blender is never more than two-thirds full and the lid is on securely. Purée the soup in batches on high speed until smooth.

Ingrid Bergman's daughter Isabella Rossellini once said, "I love *Casablanca* for the humour. It's recognised as a romantic film but there is a lightness and comical tone that is extraordinary."

Transfer the puréed soup back to the pot and whisk in the cream, crème fraîche, and nutmeg. Season with salt and pepper to taste. Simmer for an additional 4 to 5 minutes. If necessary, thin the soup out with more broth. The ideal texture should be smooth and velvety, not lumpy or gluey.

Remove from the heat, cover, and allow the soup to cool to room temperature. Then transfer to a large bowl, cover with plastic wrap, and chill in the refrigerator for 1 to 2 hours or until cold.

When it's time to serve, remove the bowl from the refrigerator. If it has separated a bit (this is normal), give it a stir until it's smooth again. Divide the soup into shot glasses or other small serving vessels and garnish each with a small dollop of crème fraîche, chopped chives, and croutons (if using). Serve chilled. Alternatively, vichyssoise can be served hot with warm, crusty bread for dipping.

PANISSE

Rick and Louis may have begun a beautiful friendship in Casablanca, but Rick and Sam managed to maintain theirs across two continents, a global war, and one crushing heartbreak. And there's no finer way to honor such a timeless friendship than with a basket of Panisse . . . which happens to be a parfait that's perfect to share! A Marseille specialty and bartender's staple, these chickpea fritters are a crispy alternative to French fries. Seasoned with a cumin spice blend, garlic, and an array of fresh herbs, Panisse is best complemented by a glass of just about anything. It's perfect for sharing with a beautiful friend or trusted confidante!

1 teaspoon olive oil, plus more for greasing

2 cups besan or other very finely ground, powdery chickpea flour

1 teaspoon Ras El Hanout (page 153) or cumin (optional)

1 tablespoon finely chopped fresh herbs (optional)

½ teaspoon fine salt

1 teaspoon garlic paste or powder

4 cups chicken or vegetable broth

Neutral oil, such as peanut or canola oil, for frying

Flaky salt, such as fleur de sel

Freshly ground black pepper

Lemon wedges, for serving (optional)

Harissa Dipping Sauce (page 142), for serving (optional)

SPECIAL TOOLS:

9-inch square cake pan

Wire whisk

Kitchen thermometer

Air fryer (optional)

Generously grease a 9-inch square cake pan with olive oil.

In a medium saucepan, combine the olive oil, besan, ras el hanout, fresh herbs, garlic paste, and fine salt to taste. Add 2 cups of broth and whisk until the mixture is smooth, then whisk in the remaining 2 cups of broth.

Bring the mixture to a boil over medium-high heat, stirring frequently with a wire whisk, until it starts to thicken. Reduce the heat to medium-low and continue to cook, stirring frequently, for 15 to 20 minutes. The mixture will resemble a very thick porridge.

Immediately transfer the mixture into the oiled pan, using an offset spatula to smooth the top as much as possible. Let cool at room temperature for 15 minutes, then transfer to the refrigerator and let set for at least 30 minutes, or up to 2 hours.

Unmold the solidified mixture onto a parchment-lined cutting board and use a sharp knife to slice it into ¾-inch batons.

Line a plate with paper towels and set nearby.

In a cast-iron or other heavy-duty skillet, heat ½ inch of neutral oil to 375°F. If you don't have a thermometer, test the oil by throwing in a small piece of bread (it should bubble and sizzle right away). Once the oil is sufficiently hot, fry the panisses in batches, being careful not to overcrowd the pan, for 3 to 4 minutes per side, or until crisped and golden brown on the outside. Alternatively, use an air fryer, spraying the cut batons with oil and spreading them evenly across the air fryer basket. Make sure to leave space in between each baton. Cook at 400°F for about 6 minutes, then flip over and cook for another 5 to 6 minutes.

Set the finished panisses aside to drain on a paper towel–lined plate. While they are still hot, sprinkle the panisses very generously with flaky salt and freshly ground black pepper. Continue frying in batches until all the panisses have been cooked.

Serve hot, immediately, with a side of lemon wedges (for squeezing onto the panisses) and harissa dipping sauce, if desired.

ABOUT
THE AUTHORS

CASSANDRA REEDER launched her blog, The Geeky Chef, in 2008, turning fictional food and drinks from a vast array of fandoms into reality with simple and fun recipes. Since then, a series of cookbooks based on the trailblazing blog have been published, including *The Geeky Chef Cookbook* and *The Geeky Bartender Drinks*. In 2023, she released *The Unofficial Princess Bride Cookbook*, a culinary love letter to a cult classic. In 2024, she co-authored *Lyrics and Libations: The Ultimate '90s Cocktail Playlist*, a spirited tribute to the music of the '90s. When not conjuring up recipes for cookbooks inspired by fiction and pop culture, Cassandra can be found perusing the food carts in Portland, Oregon, with her husband and two kids, and dreaming of new adventures on distant shores.

S. T. BENDE is a young-adult and children's author, known for the Norse mythology series Viking Academy and The Ære Saga. She's also written books for Disney, Lucasfilm, Pixar, The Jim Henson Company, and Marvel. She lives on the West Coast, where she spends far too much time at Disneyland, and she dreams of skiing on Jotunheim and Hoth. www.stbende.com

ACKNOWLEDGMENTS

Thank you to Rolanda and Joe Conversino, especially Joe for lending me your input and expertise on one of the greatest films of all time.
As always, my love and gratitude to my husband and children. Here's looking at you, kids.
—CASSANDRA REEDER

To Papa, who spent World War II fixing B-25s on makeshift airstrips in the desert of North Africa. I'm forever grateful for your bravery, your compassion, and your amazing stories—especially the one about that impromptu flight! Thank you for inspiring our family to carry on your kindness, and for being the best guardian angel we could hope for. To my husband, whose love of classic films has brought so much joy to our family. Thank you to Lex, for letting me play in this dream-franchise, and to Warner Brothers for showcasing the power of love, duty, and sacrifice in the most beautiful way. To everyone who fights for light, love, and goodness in our world—thank you for all that you do. And to my beloved boys, who always say yes to adventure—here's looking at you, kids.

—S. T. BENDE

PROP GLOSSARY

SCALLOP-EDGED TABLE

In this book: No Questions (page 87)

WOODEN ROOM DIVIDER

In this book: Moroccan Mint Tea (page 117)

MOTHER OF PEARL CHAIR

In this book: Letters of Transit (page 69)

Part of the set design for Rick's Café American, these three pieces were imported from Morocco to use while filming in Burbank.

SILVER CHAMPAGNE BUCKET

In this book: Champagne Cocktail (page 13)

Appears in the flashback scene of Rick and Ilsa in Paris.

BACCARAT CHIPS

In this book: Shocked! (SHOCKED!) (page 77)

EXHIBITING PIANO

In this book: Play It Sam (page 53)

From the set of the *Casablanca* television show, in 1983, made to match the film set piece.

BRASS FLOOR LAMP

In this book: Gin Joint
Jaunt (page 37)

HANGING LAMP

In this book: Clever Tactical Retreat
(page 97) and Tango Delle Rose (page 71)

Both lamps were pieces from Rick's Café Americain and imported from Morocco.

BIBLIOGRAPHY

American Prohibition Museum. "Aviation Cocktail Recipe & History of the Aviation Cocktail." Accessed December 18, 2023. https://www.americanprohibitionmuseum.com/cocktails/aviation#:~:text=The%20cocktail%20was%20invented%20in,Prohibition%20and%20for%20years%20after.

American Prohibition Museum. "Gin Rickey Cocktail Recipe & History of the Gin Rickey." Accessed December 18, 2023. https://www.americanprohibitionmuseum.com/cocktails/gin-rickey.

Bacall, Lauren. *By Myself and Then Some.* New York: It Books, an imprint of HarperCollins Publishers, 2014.

Bell, Steve, and Tammy La Gorce. "Which Famous Actor Hustled Chess Games in New York City?" *The New York Times*, December 2, 2016. https://www.nytimes.com/2016/12/01/nyregion/humphrey-bogart-chess.html.

Bergman, Ingrid, and Alan Burgess. *Ingrid Bergman: My Story.* New York: Delacorte Press, 1980.

Biederman, Marcia. "Lime Rickey, Drink of Yore." *The New York Times*, August 1, 1999. https://www.nytimes.com/1999/08/01/nyregion/neighborhood-report-new-york-up-close-lime-rickey-drink-of-yore.html.

Boyd, Carolyn. "Pastis, an Iconic French Aperitif Makes a Comeback." *National Geographic*, August 11, 2021. https://www.nationalgeographic.com/travel/article/pastis-an-iconic-french-aperitif-makes-a-comeback.

"Classic Americano Cocktail Recipe - 2024." MasterClass, July 1, 2023. https://www.masterclass.com/articles/classic-americano-cocktail-recipe.

Collins, Lauren. "Seeking a Cure in France's Waters." *The New Yorker*, May 23, 2022. https://www.newyorker.com/magazine/2022/05/30/seeking-a-cure-in-frances-waters.

"The Creation of 'The Rat Pack.'" CBS News, December 13, 1999. https://www.cbsnews.com/news/the-creation-of-the-rat-pack.

Curtiz, Michael (director). 1942. *Casablanca*. United States: Warner Bros.

Difford, Simon. "Bee's Knees." Cocktail recipe by Margaret Brown ("Unsinkable Molly"), July 12, 2016. https://www.diffordsguide.com/cocktails/recipe/2144/bees-knees.

Difford, Simon. "Between the Sheets." Cocktail recipe, July 12, 2016. https://www.diffordsguide.com/cocktails/recipe/209/between-the-sheets.

Difford, Simon. "Blood and Sand Cocktail." Cocktail recipe, August 29, 2014. https://www.diffordsguide.com/encyclopedia/510/cocktails/blood-and-sand-cocktail.

Difford, Simon. "Champs-Elysees Cocktail." Cocktail recipe, May 26, 2016. https://www.diffordsguide.com/cocktails/recipe/396/champs-elysees-cocktail.

Difford, Simon. "Kir and Kir Royale Cocktail." Cocktail recipe, January 22, 2021. https://www.diffordsguide.com/encyclopedia/460/cocktails/kir-and-kir-royale-cocktail.

Difford, Simon. "Martini History." Martini history, June 18, 2018. https://www.diffordsguide.com/g/1121/martini/martini-history. See also: "The Essential Martini." *The New York Times*, October 31, 1979, https://www.nytimes.com/1979/10/31/archives/the-essential-martini.html; and Fabricant, Florence. "The Martini: Stirred, Shaken or Eaten." *The New York Times*, December 4, 1996, https://www.nytimes.com/1996/12/04/garden/the-martini-stirred-shaken-or-eaten.html.

Difford, Simon. "New York Sour Cocktail." Cocktail recipe, August 2, 2018. https://www.diffordsguide.com/cocktails/recipe/3398/new-york-sour-cocktail.

Difford, Simon. "Suffering Bastard." Cocktail recipe by Joe Scialom, January 13, 2016. https://www.diffordsguide.com/cocktails/recipe/2588/suffering-bastard.

Discography of American Historical Recordings, "Brunswick Matrix CH115-CH117. It Had to Be You / Isham Jones Orchestra." Accessed May 2024. https://adp.library.ucsb.edu/index.php/matrix/detail/2000234812/Ch115-Ch117-It_had_to_be_you.

Discography of American Historical Recordings, "Gramophone matrix BD4795. Il tango delle rose / Daniele Serra." Accessed May 2024. https://adp.library.ucsb.edu/index.php/matrix/detail/1000016573/BD4795-Il_tango_delle_rose.

Fleming, Ian. "The Girl From Headquarters." *In Casino Royale*. New York: Macmillan, 1953.

Friedrich, Otto. "Opinion: How They Made the Greatest Movie in History." *The Washington Post*, February 1, 1987. https://www.washingtonpost.com/archive/opinions/1987/02/01/how-they-made-the-greatest-movie-in-history/22879d03-0b1f-4951-943b-2fc284ecafdb.

Geiling, Natasha. "The Widow Who Created the Champagne Industry." *Smithsonian*. November 5, 2013. https://www.smithsonianmag.com/arts-culture/the-widow-who-created-the-Champagne-industry-180947570.

Hamilton, William L. "A 1920's Parisienne, Revived with Panache." *The New York Times*, April 28, 2002. https://www.nytimes.com/2002/04/28/style/shaken-and-stirred-a-1920-s-parisienne-revived-with-panache.html.

Harmetz, Aljean. *The Making of 'Casablanca': Bogart, Bergman, and World War II*. New York, New York: Hyperion, 2002.

Isenberg, Noah. "In 'Casablanca,' Madeleine Lebeau Became Forever the Face of French Resistance." *Humanities* 38, no. 1, 2017. https://www.neh.gov/humanities/2017/winter/feature/in-casablanca-madeleine-lebeau-became-forever-the-face-french-resistance.

Isenberg, Noah. *We'll Always Have Casablanca: The Life, Legend, and Afterlife of Hollywood's Most Beloved Movie*. London: Faber and Faber, 2020.

Larsen, Ernest. *The Usual Suspects*. London: BFI, 2005.

Lebo, Harlan. *'Casablanca': Behind the Scenes*. New York: Simon & Schuster, 1992.

Lee, Lanee. "Drink in History: Kir Royale." *Chilled Magazine*, May 14, 2023. https://chilledmagazine.com/drink-in-history-kir-royale.

Library of Congress. "Research Guides: World War II: A Resource Guide." Accessed May 2024. https://guides.loc.gov/ww2/library-of-congress-resources.

Margolick, David. "The Creator of Rick's Cafe Seeks Rights to 'Casablanca' Characters." *The New York Times*, October 10, 1985. https://www.nytimes.com/1985/10/10/nyregion/the-creator-of-rick-s-cafe-seeks-rights-to-casablanca-characters.html?pagewanted=all.

"A Message from Jessica Rains." Park Ridge Classic Film, March 15, 2014. https://parkridgeclassicfilm.com/2014/03/15/a-message-from-jessica-rains.

The National Constitution Center. "6.5 Primary Source: Montesquieu, the Spirit of the Laws (1748)." Accessed May 2024. https://constitutioncenter.org/education/classroom-resource-library/classroom/6.5-primary-source-montesquieu-the-spirit-of-the-laws.

"1937 Café Royal Cocktail Book Coronation Edition 18." Compiled by W. J. Tarling. Euvs Vintage Cocktail Books, 1937. https://euvs-vintage-cocktail-books.cld.bz/1937-Cafe-Royal-Cocktail-Book-Coronation-Edition/18.

"Not Proud of His Honors." *The Wellsboro Gazette*, July 26, 1901, and *Mansfield News*, July 7, 1900. https://yesteryearsnews.wordpress.com/2009/06/20/joe-rickey-a-man-and-a-drink.

Peppler, Rebekah. "A French 75 for Everyone." *The New York Times*, January 21, 2022. https://www.nytimes.com/2022/01/21/dining/drinks/french-75-cocktails.html.

Rossellini, Isabella. "Isabella Rossellini: Remembering Mamma with These Five Films." A.Frame. Accessed May 2024. https://aframe.oscars.org/what-to-watch/post/remembering-mamma-with-these-five-films.

Simonson, Robert. "Celebrating the Roaring 2020s with a Bee's Knees Cocktail." *The New York Times*, February 2, 2023. https://www.nytimes.com/2023/02/02/dining/drinks/bees-knees-cocktail.html.

Van Gelder, Lawrence. "Leonid Kinskey, 95, Bartender in 'Casablanca.'" *The New York Times*, September 12, 1998. https://www.nytimes.com/1998/09/12/movies/leonid-kinskey-95-bartender-in-casablanca.html.

Whittaker, Richard. "Five Films about Our Favorite Bartenders." *The Austin Chronicle*, July 13, 2018. https://www.austinchronicle.com/screens/2018-07-13/five-films-about-our-favorite-bartenders.

INSIGHT
EDITIONS

PO Box 3088
San Rafael, CA 94912
www.insighteditions.com

Find us on Facebook: www.facebook.com/InsightEditions
Follow us on Instagram: @insighteditions

ISBN: 979-8-88663-772-4

Publisher: Raoul Goff
SVP, Group Publisher: Vanessa Lopez
VP, Creative: Chrissy Kwasnik
VP, Manufacturing: Alix Nicholaeff
Editorial Director: Thom O'Hearn
Art Director: Stuart Smith
Designer: Brooke McCullum
Editor: Alexis Sattler
Editorial Assistant: Anna Friedman
VP, Senior Executive Project Editor: Vicki Jaeger
Production Manager: Deena Hashem
Strategic Production Planner: Lina s Palma-Temena

Photography by Lindsay Kreighbaum
Drink and food styling by Bianca Swanepoel
Prop styling by Aimie Vredevoogd

ROOTS of PEACE ⊕ REPLANTED PAPER

Insight Editions, in association with Roots of Peace, will plant two trees for each tree used in the manufacturing of this book. Roots of Peace is an internationally renowned humanitarian organization dedicated to eradicating land mines worldwide and converting war-torn lands into productive farms and wildlife habitats. Roots of Peace will plant two million fruit and nut trees in Afghanistan and provide farmers there with the skills and support necessary for sustainable land use.

Manufactured in China by Insight Editions

10 9 8 7 6 5 4 3 2 1